ADVANCED PARALLEL PROGRAMMING

AND THE

LAW OF ATTRACTION

How to Share the Law of Attraction
and Bring Abundance to the People You Love

Dr. Richard K. Nongard

R.J. Banks

www.AdvancedParallelProgramming.com

ADVANCED PARALLEL PROGRAMMING and the LAW OF ATTRACTION:

How to Share the Law of Attraction and Bring Abundance to the People You Love

By Dr. Richard K. Nongard and R.J. Banks

Copyright © 2019 Dr. Richard K. Nongard and R.J. Banks

First Printing: January 2020

ISBN-13: 978-1-7344678-0-2

Published by:
Subliminal Science Press
15560 N. Frank L. Wright Blvd. B4-118
Scottsdale, AZ 85260

(702) 418-3332

www.NongardBooks.com
www.AdvancedParallelProgramming.com

Dr. Richard Nongard and R.J. Banks are available to speak at your business or conference event on a variety of topics. Call (702) 418-3332 for booking information.

What Others are Saying:

"Dr. Richard Nongard and R.J. Banks have done it again with their newest book! Advanced Parallel Programming is exactly what the world needs right now is a time where emotions and the tensions of life are at a level that could easily derail even the most positive of people looking to accomplish meaningful goals. If you have struggled with mastering the "Law of Attraction" but are now ready to taste true happiness and success by learning how to share it with others, then this is the book with the REAL secret ingredients." **-Rich Guzzi,** @guruguzzi (Entertainer and comedian with millions of followers on Twitter).

"As you read this book, you soon realize this information expands upon everything you already knew and progresses your understanding a few steps further as you move on to advance your skills and knowledge about what it truly means to practice the Law of Attraction." **– Victoria Gallagher,** Bestselling Author of *Practical Law of Attraction: Align Yourself with the Manifesting Conditions and Successfully Attract Your Desires*

"As a leading teacher of the Law of Attraction, people often ask me, "How can I share abundance and prosperity with others?" This book not only shows you how, but also how to create alignment that will make the world a better place!" - **Dr. Steve G. Jones,** Television Personality and Author

Why Read this Book?

This book focuses on taking your knowledge and practice of the Law of Attraction and advancing it to a level where you can discover sustained success and reap abundance in every area of your life. When you finish this book, you will know exactly how to use the method of Advanced Parallel Programming to unleash your greatest level of potential.

This book is a step-by-step guidebook for using the principles of the Law of Attraction in your health, your wealth, and your habits. It will show you how to protect yourself from negative influences and teach you to thrive, even when facing uphill battles with those who should be most supportive. Most importantly, it will show you how you can influence others in a positive way and create a powerful circle of power by sharing the Law of Attraction with others.

Are you ready to reap the power the Law of Attraction offers, and also ready to lift up those around you so they can share in your success? Read this book and you will enter an advanced level of success and create alignment wherever you go, allowing yourself to make not only your world, but everyone's world, a better place.

TABLE OF CONTENTS

ABOUT THE AUTHORS

Dr. Richard K. Nongard is an ICBCH Certified Professional Hypnotist, a Licensed Marriage and Family Therapist and an expert in helping people create lasting success. He has been a TEDx speaker, he is a popular author with over 20 books to his credit, and his self-hypnosis videos have been viewed by more than four million people.

Dr. Richard K. Nongard is the expert other professionals come to study with to learn advanced methods of professional hypnosis, Advanced Parallel Programming, and the Law of Attraction. In this book, he reveals the strategies that actually work and shows you how you can do them at home. Everything is explained in step-by-step detail. When you are finished with this book, you will have a new resource that you can tap into for the rest of your life.

i

Dr. Richard Nongard is a popular conference and keynote speaker, known for his relaxed and engaging style. His focus is on real-world solutions based on the science of leadership. His presentations focus on leadership, engagement and actionable strategies for business success. He holds a Doctorate in Transformational Leadership (Cultural Transformation) from Bakke Graduate University and a master's degree in counseling from Liberty University.

Richard is the author of numerous books, publications, and training videos. His book on leadership, *Viral Leadership: Seize the Power of Now to Create Lasting Transformation in Business*, has already become a popular resource for leadership development. He has written many other books as well, including psychology textbooks that have been adapted as textbooks at the university level, and his 5-star reviews are a testament to the value Richard provides in both written and spoken media.

Dr. Richard K. Nongard is a coach, consultant and leadership development expert, offering services to business groups, sales groups and other organizations. You can bring him to your organization to train your executives or front-line employees in Viral Leadership, Self-Hypnosis, and the Law of Attraction.

Do you want Dr. Richard K. Nongard or R.J. Banks to be the motivational speaker at your next event? Call (702) 418-3332 or visit NONGARD.com

Robert (R.J.) Banks is a lover of wisdom and a passionate student of life. He has discovered the true joy and happiness that arrives from serving and helping others through inspiring and empowering millions to live their greatest lives. In his continued studies and experiences, he embodies and shares his knowledge and interpretation of inspired optimal living and co-creating the happy life we all deserve.

Having been taught the Law of Attraction at an early age, R.J. has been blessed with an exciting and adventurous life. While proudly serving in the US Air Force, he was handpicked to join the USAF Thunderbirds air demonstration team. His post-military endeavors led him to Hollywood and the entertainment industry where he spent the next twelve years as a radio DJ, a recording studio owner, a music producer and professional musician. In his early forties, R.J. further elevated his service to others by entering the medical field as a Diagnostic Imaging Specialist.

In 2013, R.J.'s life took an unexpected turn when he was diagnosed with an "inoperable" brain tumor. Within a very short time he had lost most everything in the material world.

He could no longer work in radiology, he lost his six-figure income, his beautiful house at the local country club, all his fancy cars, his wife left, and he was told he only had 6 to 8 months to live. By using the power of the Law of Attraction, R.J. was blessed with finding a neurosurgeon who could perform the delicate brain surgery. Although the surgery was a success, R.J. is now blind. But, he is also the happiest he has ever been in his life!

Through this challenge and leading up to his surgery, R.J. became self-inspired and self-motivated to create his now-famous LOA Affirmations audio programs. During this time, he wrote his bestselling book, *The Power of I Am and the Law of Attraction*. Within its pages, instead of using philosophical words explaining the meaning of the power of, "I AM" and the "Law of Attraction," he gives the reader practical steps on how to discover the natural power that is hidden within all of us. R.J. reveals where to find it, how to develop and refine it, and how to use it at will for whatever one truly desires.

After spending the next 4 years recovering from brain surgery and learning how to live as a blind person, R.J. and his guide dog, Cabo, now reside in Las Vegas, Nevada, where he spends his time as a writer, a cognitive behavioral therapist, and a voice-over recording artist.

With over a half million followers on Facebook, (www.facebook.com/loaaffirmations), R.J. is happily using and sharing his knowledge and experience with the power of the I AM and the Law of Attraction to help others break the cycle of being pulled and pushed by their own unknown commands of the Law of Attraction. He is currently in the final stages of completing his next book titled, *New Beginnings, and The Law of Attraction*, which details starting one's life over after experiencing sudden adversity.

Contact R.J. at <u>www.RobBanksVoiceovers.com</u>

FOREWORD

By Victoria M Gallagher, the #1 Best Selling Author of *Practical Law of Attraction, Align Yourself with the Manifesting Conditions and Successfully Attract Your Desires:*

You've undoubtedly heard about the Law of Attraction.

You've painstakingly read books and watched movies and videos on YouTube about the topic.

You've honed your manifesting skills.

Maybe you've even manifested a few things already. Big things. Small things.

You've developed the habit of meditation.

You have mastered dozens of techniques to help you keep your vibration high.

Why doesn't it stay that way?

Why is it so hard to create lasting and permanent change in this area?

You've told yourself things like; "If I could just maintain that positive, high vibrational state of mind, life would be wonderful!"

You'd be right to think so. You'd become a manifesting machine. You'd be happier, healthier, and more abundant.

What is that thing that takes you out of the vibration you work so hard to develop?

Even though you strive to keep your vibration high, when you're tuned in to one frequency and the people you are surrounded by are tuned into another, it can undermine your efforts to focus on the positive things you desire.

Being surrounded by negativity can be a debilitating problem and hinder your chances of success.

This is something which seldom gets talked about.

On the other hand, you may already be at a point in your life where you've enjoyed lots of success with attracting abundance, prosperity, and well-being. Because of the positive experiences you've had how well it's been working, you're excited and feel compelled to give heartfelt advice to your friends, your family, and your peers. You try to help. You know if only they would try to be a bit more positive, their lives would improve. You share your insight. You let them in on your little secret. You generously impart your wisdom, only to have this insight fall completely on deaf ears. Heck, I know I've experienced this situation with so many people, as far back to when I first started applying it.

"Oh, that's so great for you, Victoria!" They say as they continue on their merry way, doing what they've always done and complaining about what they always get in return.

As you read through these pages and begin using Advanced Parallel Programming and The Law of Attraction, you'll finally get why the people in your life don't change or adapt their communication style to a more positive way of thinking. It becomes abundantly clear why they don't listen to your advice. You'll then learn effective strategies that do work to influence your friends and loved ones to become curious about how they too can empower themselves to create the desirable results you've always wanted for them.

There are possibly hundreds of books that teach you what the Law of Attraction is and how to apply it in your life. I have thoroughly done my research and I can assure you, there is no other book dedicated to such an altruistic approach on what to do when you're on this path and the rest of your world is not.

This book goes beyond the typical 'what's in it for me' approach. It kicks it up to a whole new all-encompassing level by having the reader realize that we have a responsibility to come from abundance. It's natural to want us all to succeed. The way to get there is to lead by example. Everything in the universe, including all of our thoughts, feelings, and vibration is energy. Though we may seem separate, we are very much connected. Like it or not, other people have the ability to influence us. Yet, the reverse is true as well.

Advanced Parallel Programming embarks on very specific territory that no other book on the Law of Attraction goes into any depth about.

How to practice The Law of Attraction in an environment that mocks positivity is an essential skill to the serious student who wishes to utilize and practice getting favorable results.

I believe Richard and R.J. created a new category here in this unique and relevant manual which gives the reader a true sense of completion to the already existing LOA process. It works wonderfully well as a complement to any of the existing books that are on the market today.

For those who are new to Law of Attraction, you'll be given a brief practical summary of what the Law of Attraction is and how to apply it.

You'll be moved by inspirational stories, which are a testament to the fact that it not only works for some people, but it can work for anyone.

Practical tips are given on strategies to protect ourselves from our well-meaning friends and relatives.

This book tells you the truth you really need to hear in a straightforward, hard-hitting, yet compassionate way.

Simple, yet cutting edge strategies to protect yourself from a negative world, utilizing their signature "Bubble of Protection" Techniques; C.O.R.E., L.O.V.E., and F.U.N.

Each acronym and their letters provide effective practices you can apply to the different elements of your life to help you raise your vibration, and protect yourself from the negativity which undoubtedly exists, but you don't always need to pay attention to it. This book walks you through the steps you can take to cut the garbage out of your life, and make room for positive, inspiring, and helpful resources which you'll find in abundance, if only you choose to take a look from a new perspective.

Richard Nongard is an influential author with a depth of understanding in the personal growth arena. He contributes vital information to the world of Law of Attraction to greatly enhance your experience when it comes to its application in your life.

The collaboration with R.J. Banks, who's insights and inspirational messages have already changed the lives of hundreds of thousands of fans and followers over the years, makes getting this book a must-read for Law of Attraction enthusiasts or, quite frankly, anyone who wishes to empower themselves and others to improve their life.

As you read this book, you soon realize this information expands upon everything you already knew and progresses your understanding a few steps further as you move on to advance your skills and knowledge about what it truly means to practice the Law of Attraction.

In the final sections, as if your mind hasn't been stretched enough, you'll be introduced to even more profound knowledge of how the Law of Attraction works at the universal level. Each section and each chapter of this book is significant, life-changing, and takes you on a profound and thoughtful journey.

In the closing, you'll dive into the skills you'll need to use on a daily basis to enhance your imagination and visualization.

I see this book as a must-read, one which you'll come back to again and again until it becomes imprinted at the subconscious level of your mind.

I appreciate the insightful, inspiring, and refreshing viewpoint on a subject so near and dear to my heart.

Thank you, Richard and R.J. for the honor and privilege of sharing my thoughts with your readers.

Victoria M. Gallagher, #1 Selling author of *Practical Law of Attraction: Align Yourself with the Manifesting Conditions and Successfully Attract Your Desires*

Visit **HypTalk.com** to learn more about Victoria and her powerful self-help books.

Dr. Richard K. Nongard and R.J. Banks

SECTION ONE:

THE IMPORTANCE OF ALIGNMENT

Chapter One:
Advanced Parallel Programming

What would happen if railroad tracks were not parallel? Well, obviously, the train would never make it down the track and might even derail. What would a tennis match be like if the court lines were not parallel? Would it be a fair game? Would your window go up and down smoothly if the edges were not parallel? Of course not. Even this book requires parallel lines; without them, the words would simply slide off the page.

The Law of Attraction (LOA) is like a railway system in that it requires a state of parallel programming to smoothly guide your success. If you wish to manifest health, but start your morning with jelly doughnuts, and end your days with a candy bar, your desires and your actions are not on a parallel track. If you want to achieve financial security, but you are out playing slot machines at a casino every week, the issue when you run short at the end of the month is not a failure of the Law of Attraction, but a lack of alignment between your goals and your actions.

Hollywood movies, TV shows, concert halls, sports arenas and top-level corporations are filled with people who attribute their success to the Law of Attraction. People like Will Smith, Jim Carrey, Lady Gaga, Mark Cuban and Mel Robbins (just to name a few) all allowed the Law of Attraction to guide them in one way or another.

There is also a list of very talented people, but these are the people whom you've never heard of. Who are these people? These are the people who have allowed the undesirable effects of the Law of Attraction to dominate their lives because of their own limiting beliefs.

You don't have to be a celebrity in order to reap the benefits of Advanced Parallel Programming and the Law of Attraction. The celebrities previously mentioned began their journey with nothing but hope, desire and a relentless drive. These factors influenced the Law of Attraction to their advantage. And you can do the same. It doesn't matter where or how you were raised; it is your *choice* as to how you will live from this day forward.

This book focuses on taking your knowledge and practice of LOA and advancing it to a level where you can create protection for yourself while around those with negative attitudes. It will also teach you to influence others so they can also see the desirable attributes of LOA and how they too can choose to enhance their lives.

A perfect example of this process is the story of Roger Roan Eagle. Roger is a Lakota Native American born and raised on the Pine Ridge Indian reservation in South Dakota. Like so many others raised in this kind of repressed environment, Roger grew up in an abusive family filled with violence, drug and alcohol abuse. Shortly after his abusive father abandoned them and his mother died, he, like most other high-risk youths, was jostled from foster home to foster home, abusive and uncaring relatives and eventually onto the streets, struggling in an attempt to escape this life.

Sadly, it wasn't long before Roger found himself with the same addictions and violent behavior he tried so desperately to escape. This, unfortunately, is a very common outcome for many Native Americans. After many years of living this way, Roger decided it was time to turn his life around. Working with nothing but his intuition and inner-self, he stopped doing drugs, stopped drinking alcohol, and began his quest for a better, happier and more fulfilling life.

The law of attraction is a vibrational energy that attracts on the same vibrational plane. It wasn't long after he decided to change that he and R.J. Banks met at an Indian pow-wow in Seattle. R.J.'s mother is Lakota as well. Soon, the two became brothers (in the sacred term) and ever since, Roger has become a very well-known Native American artist. He creates beautiful, authentic Lakota dreamcatchers and jewelry. As if that isn't enough, he is a disciple of the Law of Attraction.

Over the last few years, Roger has helped countless others on their quests for a better, happier, and more fulfilling life. He returns to Pine Ridge and other reservations, inspiring others and helping change their lives. He also goes on keynote speaking engagements with R.J. and tells his story of hope and encouragement. Roger Roan Eagle is a true inspiration. His use of Advanced Parallel Programming and the Law of Attraction is spot on. He focuses on what he desires, he shields himself from the undesirable, and he leads and lives by example. He welcomes, encourages and helps any and all that desire to turn their lives around.

When it comes to the Law of Attraction, one often hears doubts and disbelief. We believe, and it is scientifically proven, the LOA is just like any other law of the universe. One cannot see electricity, but one knows it's there. It can light your home (desirable effect) or it can kill you (undesirable effect). When it comes to the Law of Attraction, this undesirable effect is often jokingly played off as Murphy's Law— "whatever can go wrong, will go wrong," as well as the good ole adages like "If it weren't for bad luck, I'd have no luck at all." Although these are cute and witty sayings that will most likely get you a chuckle or two, the damage you are doing to yourself is unconsciously overpowering and defeating to one's self-worth. Lesson one:

Stop self-criticizing, even if you're joking! Your subconscious does not know the difference and will believe and follow what you tell it to.

There is also a common saying, how one cannot change another person or situation, but can change how one chooses to react to these undesirable situations and/ or people. This is the kind of thinking that limits our full potential. Yes, there will be those who refuse to participate in our good fortune, but even the most skeptical around will respond positively to our desires to share abundance if we have the right tools to share, communicate with the right spirit, and have set an example for prosperity that serves as a beacon for awareness.

We are going to give you a new ability by teaching you what we have taught thousands of others: how to stop thinking in one direction and acting in another. The examples so far have been fairly simplistic, but as you read through them you can see how important parallel programming is. The skill we will teach you in this book is what we call Advanced Parallel Programming (APP) because it goes far beyond the simple solutions, such as: if you want health, eat right; if you want wealth, spend right; and if you want happiness, do things that make you happy. These are simple roadblocks to activating your greatest potential, and it is often the simple things that hold us back from activating abundance.

Parallel Programming, interestingly, is a computer science term. It's a term that refers to running two or more programs simultaneously or stacking hardware in a way that computations are done in unison, but on different levels. The metaphor applies to our thinking, our feelings, and to our actions when applying the Law of Attraction to our everyday lives and to the lives of the people around us.

We want to take parallel programming to an advanced level in these pages. We share methods of reprogramming your own self-defeating thoughts, feelings and actions and also solve the biggest issue in creating positive alignment: the people in our everyday world that most of us face.

We live in a post-truth world. It seems that people act in ways that are destructive to happiness, destructive to success, and destructive to relationships. They do not do this because they want to have a miserable life, but rather, because they've been programmed to think this way. Limiting beliefs are instilled in us from negative messenger in almost every form of media; in our schooling, from our jobs, and surprisingly, even from the people who should be helping us like parents, spouses, and friends. Sometimes, they do this out of malevolence, but they often simply do it because they do not know truth. They do not know that wealth is possible. They do not know that health is possible, and they do not know that happiness is what has been promised to us. Many of the people we love, the people we work with, or the people we must interact with are often out of alignment with us. Our track is not parallel to their tracks. Getting those people to share a resourceful mindset is imperative if we want to create lasting success in our own lives. This is the crux of Advanced Parallel Programming. It lets us create a high vibration not only in our own lives but in the world around us.

APP is the mechanism for creating alignment between your conscious actions and your subconscious habits, alignment between your beliefs and your actions, as well as yourself and the people you are connected to. Through reading this book, you are going to explore in detail various methods to create alignment through advanced methods of creating parallel programming. You are probably familiar with methods of auto-suggestions, self-hypnosis, and positive affirmations. When used correctly, these will create alignment where, in the past, there have been misalignments. These are a part of any approach to Advanced Parallel Programming. As you progress through later chapters in this book, you will discover additional methods to create alignment, create harmony and build on your ability to create parallel programming in every aspect of your life - and in the world around you.

By sharing the desirable aspects of the Law of Attraction with others, we help ourselves. We are not islands unto ourselves. We probably will not reach our financial goals if we do not have the cooperation of our significant other. We will probably not find satisfaction as a parent, if our children do not share the same ability, we have to generate solutions. We will probably not find health if the people we surround ourselves with do not contribute to a clean environment and function as stewards of the environment.

To really create abundance, success, and manifest our dreams, desires, and goals, we must operate in a world where others exist and are a part of our lives. What they think, feel and do will directly impact us and our world. To truly hone the Law of Attraction, we must share the Law of Attraction, and use our strength to create unity among others.

The Law of Divine Oneness refers to the axiom that everything is interconnected. In popular culture, this is known as *The Butterfly Effect*. If one person takes an action somewhere, in one way or another, that action will impact us. In science, Sir Isaac Newton called our world a *Clockwork Universe*, meaning that nothing happens by chance and every mechanism in the universe impacts every other mechanism's ability to function. If your grandparents moved to rural America 100 years ago, your family probably lives in the same city, and there is a high probability you do too. Your past brought you to where you are today because of its interconnectedness to the present.

The Law of Divine Oneness is expressed in family therapy through the concept of genograms. This refers to the idea that when a psychological and social family tree is mapped, families tend to repeat themselves. Now think about your family. While it might be amazing in some ways, there is also a great likelihood that what happened in your family's history is harshing the present satisfaction you have with your life. At its core, people are out of alignment. They are not running on a parallel program with us. Our tracks often don't align. And this is what's holding you back.

Have you been practicing positive self-talk, meditation or prayer, and affirmations and feeling a high vibration only to have your happiness and abundance buzz killed by the lack of support you get from others? Do people even make fun of you for trying to create a better life and really understanding the Law of Attraction?

We recently ate lunch with a friend, who lamented "Just when I feel like everything is going my way, someone or something comes and takes it away." This is not an uncommon observation people make. Have you felt this way at one point or another?

With this book, you will create an Advanced Parallel Program in your own thinking, feelings and action so that you have congruence between what you want and what you do. We will tackle the self-talk that is self-defeating, and how the Law of Attraction can help you manifest successes when we overcome our own worst enemy – ourselves. We are going to focus on helping you to "level-up," while also helping you to help your friends, your family, your coworkers and even your community.

Marianne Williamson said it this way, "Each of us has a unique part to play in healing the world." We hope that this book not only makes your world a better place, but that it makes all of our worlds a better place. This will happen when we not only create a parallel program between our conscious and subconscious minds, but also when we advance it to the next level and create this alignment in others around us. By following the laws of attraction that "like attracts Like," the Six Degrees of separation phenomenon (the mathematical formula that we are all socially connected by no more than six people) will eventually connect us all together harmoniously and will create a better world for all of us

Of course, there are those who do not want to have any part in positivity, abundance, a better world, or the Law of Attraction. These are the unfortunate people, and might even be the very people we care about deeply, and will remain connected to either by choice or necessity. In this case, it is important that we create a shield from negativity, scarcity thinking, and a mindset of confidence. We will teach you those strategies as well.

Are you ready to manifest abundance in your own life and passionately share that with the world around you? Then read on and learn how to get your mental railroad tracks in alignment with your actions, shield yourself from the doubts of others, and make the world a better place through Advanced Parallel Programming and the Law of Attraction. You'll be glad you did!

Chapter Two:
Back to Basics

Many of you have purchased this book as an academic means of advancing your knowledge and skills managing the Law of Attraction.

In a world full of "armchair experts and professionals," it is the real-world "boots on the ground" soldier that is at the forefront cutting the pathways and making advances in any field. You are, without a doubt, one of these soldiers learning, pushing, striving at your craft, becoming better and more advanced.

To begin your journey into the next level of Advanced Parallel Programming and the Law of Attraction, we begin with a brief review of the Law of Attraction. Please don't skip over this chapter, even if you think you already know this stuff, it's important to review and understand deeply.

As a comparison, music has many components for every song: The melody, the lyrics, the timing, tempo, key etc. In addition, when one performs in a band, there are additional *Synchronous* components, i.e. everyone has to be playing the same song, in the same key and at the same tempo and timing in order to get the desired result of a stellar performance. A seasoned professional musician, when preparing to perform, will review the songs structure, even if they have performed it countless times for many years. This brings back into focus the components of the song so that the desired outcome is an amazing performance. The Law of Attraction *theoretically* shares many aspects of this same component matrix.

The foundation of the Law of Attraction has been refined to the rudimentary equation of "Ask, Believe and Receive." Although this does hold true in the fundamental, one soon learns both the mindset and the process can be a bit more complex.

In his book, *The Power of I Am and The Law of Attraction*, R.J. Banks explains the importance of getting one's head into the right state of mind as the pre-step to Ask, Believe and Receive. The key mindsets he, as well as many other professionals, recommends are:

1. Happiness
2. Gratitude
3. Worthiness

Happiness:

It is well researched and documented that when asked the question "What do you want?" the most popular answer, worldwide, is "happiness." This is also the most popular answer when parents are asked what they want most for their children. It is widely accepted and understood that happiness is the driving force behind many of our life goals, such as success, prosperity, wellness and loving relationships.

Happiness is our natural state of being and is something that we already are and always will be, yet so many people spend much of their lives searching for happiness. Does this sound familiar? – "I will be happy when _____." Happiness is not an external "thing" that you can get, buy, earn, or find. It is not a by-product or reward of achievement. Happiness is what we define as an essence of being and something that we already "are." Think of "happiness" as the sun. On a cloudy day, we commonly, yet erroneously say "the sun is not shining today." But the sun is, in fact, shining. The sun is always shining; we just don't see it from where we are because a cloud is blocking it. When we choose to move out from under the cloud, we are once again in the sunshine. If you are not living in happiness, you have the choice to stay where you are, or move out from under the cloud and into happiness.

Gratitude:

You've heard and read countless times that gratitude is the shortest path to happiness. The more grateful you are, the happier you will feel, and happiness combined with sincere gratitude opens the door to abundance! Yes, you read it correctly! If you want to attract incredibly desirable things into your life, start by showing your gratitude, love and appreciation to all the people and things you already have around you. This is not a one-time "thanks," or a weekly, monthly or annual "Thanksgiving" appreciation speech or acknowledgment list. It is a daily, hourly, ongoing exhibit. Your display of gratitude should be constant so it can become a way of life. Remember, 'like attracts like' and the more you show your gratitude and appreciation, the more you will be appreciated.

Here are some ways to start practicing gratitude to improve your well-being:

1. Keep a gratitude journal. At the beginning and end of each day, write down 3-5 things from the day you feel grateful for. Simplicity is key. Your baby's smile, a perfect sunset, the train arriving on time, or your best friend's laughter. Relish the feeling you get when remembering and writing it down.
2. Express your gratitude. Take the time to share your feelings. Not the simple, polite "thank you," but the real and heartfelt emotions. Tell your friend how her support and sense of humor helps you get through tough times,

15

and how much it means to you. Don't take your loved ones for granted. Let them know how much you love them and why.

3. Look for what is right about a situation, not what's wrong. Sure you're frustrated by the bus being late, but thankfully you have an understanding boss. Service at the restaurant is poor, but you are lucky to afford an evening out surrounded by good friends.

Worthiness:

You must have a rock-solid, indestructible, unshakable and secure sense of self-worth. Your own self-worth will determine whether you will succeed or fail in creating your desires in life.

You must feel worthy and deserving of a grand and miraculous lifestyle. Your true emotional beliefs are nestled deep within your subconscious mind and are developed over time. Henry Ford stated, *"Whether you think you can or think you can't, you're absolutely right."* Thinking *"I can't"* is, in our opinion, the purest and truest form of self-imposed limitations caused by your lack of self-worth. The bottom line is: How you feel about yourself is a choice, even if it often doesn't feel that way.

Your First Level of Applying Advanced Parallel Programming:

Getting your mindset in sync with your desires

In our perceived reality, there are several vibrational energies that transmit outside of your human sensory receptors. The Law of Attraction is one of them. Much like ultrasonic frequencies, infrared light, and magnetic force field's, thought vibrations are, and have been scientifically proven, to be an amazing phenomenon that functions outside of our sensory spectrum. EVERYTHING in its purest and most basic form is comprised of energy that constantly emits a frequency. We all transmit and receive with our thoughts. Harnessing and using this energy to our favor is the task at hand. You don't have to know or even understand the "how" of thought vibrations, you simply need to understand that this energy is yours to use in a controlled way. Think of electricity. Most of us have no idea "how" it really works, we just plug something in, flip a switch, and it works. What about a radio, television, the internet or your cell phone? We just use these forms of technology and don't think of the how they are working. Knowing, believing and controlling thought vibrations is, in our opinion, one of the most critical elements of the LOA.

Your thought energy, or vibrations, determines what you attract and experience in every facet of your life. Whether it happens consciously or not, *like attracts like*. By broadcasting (and receiving) specific thought frequencies, you broadcast into the universe and then attract the people, places, situations, opportunities, circumstances and things parallel to your thought vibrations.

This is why it is so important to be and stay happy no matter what your current situation might be. Always show gratitude to and for everything and everyone, know you are worthy, and remember that focus equals fuel. Your past is behind you; choose to keep it there. When you are driving your car, take a moment to notice how huge the windshield is compared to the rearview mirror, and there's a reason for that. Life is always moving forward, so you should also stay focused on moving forward.

Your thought vibrations are neither good nor bad, positive or negative, they are just neutral thoughts. We are the ones who choose whether they are desirable or undesirable thoughts.

Remember: What we choose to think, say and believe about ourselves and our perceived reality becomes what we are and what we attract into our lives. Focus equals fuel; where your attention goes, energy flows.

It is common to hear people say negative things about themselves in a humorous and joking manner. You might recognize statements such as: "Through the lips and straight to the hips" or "Well if it weren't for bad luck I'd have no luck at all." Although these statements are funny, you have got to realize your subconscious mind does not have a sense of humor and does not know that you are just joking around. To your subconscious, your words are an affirmation that it takes literally, and then it goes to work to broadcast the necessary thought frequencies to attract your affirmation. So, after your negative thought process, your desires have been fulfilled…welcome the weight gain and the bad luck! You asked for it and the universe delivered, just as you affirmed. All sarcasm aside, you are the creator of your own reality.

When you function on your high vibrational level, you notice that most people, and even animals, respond well to you. You're not inclined to encounter many issues or problems, and you may even stumble upon a bit of good luck that you wouldn't normally expect. When operating from a higher level of thought vibration, people may subconsciously pick up on the fact that you are giving out what the Beach Boys sang about: "Good Vibrations!"

Stay conscious of your thoughts and check yourself regularly, as in every hour. The key is to train your thinking to stay in a high vibrational frequency.

When focusing on one's desires, many ask themselves three questions:

1. What do I want?
2. How do I get it?
3. When do I get it?

Question number one: The toughest question in the world for many people to answer is "What are your life's desires?" Not wishes or hopes, but the true desires and passions that exceed everything else in your life.

Once you have created the list of your true desires, it's time to answer the next question within that question, and that is simply…why? Yes, the question is: why? Why are these things, be they material, emotional, spiritual or psychological, on your list?

We have found there are two types of answers. The first type of answer is a truly heartfelt reason as to why you desire what you desire, and the other type of reason might seem more acquisitive or egocentric. If you can't feel it in your heart and soul, then it may be an ego-driven desire. Now, you can use this information to learn a little more about yourself and what motivates you, and of course, *why*.

Once you strip away all of the ego-driven, superficial and or society induced brainwashing and programmed reasons, you will find the core reason for your true desires is to be happy and to spread and share that joy with others.

Now, this is where it really starts to get exciting! You've learned that happiness is the ultimate quest in life and the key reason that motivates us to do just about everything we do. So, the question "what are your life's desires" is really asking: "what influences your happiness?"

As you have read in the previous chapter, happiness is always with you, it just gets clouded over from time to time. So, if you are already happy, why do you desire the things on your list? We believe the fundamental reasons behind these desires is the key, the secret, the missing or hidden ingredient! And the answer is: *"You don't need them to make you happy!"* When you *need* something, you are informing and convincing your inner self, or subconscious, the universe and your higher power that you are choosing to feel or "be" incomplete or in a state of lacking. When you feel this way, you broadcast and therefore receive on a low vibrational plain, and will continue to feel the sense of lack and our present reality

As stated many times throughout historic teachings, everything in our physical world is first manifested in an imaginary or vibrational plane. From there, things manifest into the physical plain. Therefore, once we learn to enjoy our life in the visionary plane, we have committed to its fruition in the physical plain. By doing so, we project only high vibrational emotions toward the desire and don't transmit any feelings of lack.

We are however, blessed with a physical world and the power to manifest our desires into the physical in order to enhance and share our pleasures and happiness. Once this concept is realized, you can flourish in your high vibrational or visionary reality within your imagination and truly feel the joy and happiness the desire stimulates. Once you learn to maintain this high vibrational level of being, you will be presented with opportunities to take action that will manifest your desires into your physical reality.

The fine art of asking is definitely a learned process that becomes developed and refined throughout our lives. When it comes to the Law of Attraction and universal, higher or divine powers, the art of asking can be puzzling. As we have learned already, the law of attraction is a constant and it's a force that is always working behind the curtain, so to speak, to manifest our desires. Your subconscious mind is the driving power source behind this proverbial curtain. You have also learned that what you think about the most, you attract into our life. Remember: We are and attract into our lives what we choose to think, say and believe about ourselves and our perceived reality.

In his book, *As a Man Thinketh,* James Allen writes that the mere act of being who we are and the vibrational plain we emulate is a rudimentary and peripheral way of asking for our desires to manifest into the physical. *Asking by being* is the essence of the Law of Attraction, and although this act in and of itself will produce physically manifested results, there are additional, more refined ways of asking that can assist in manifesting more desirable results.

When it comes to detailing your desires, there are many schools of thought regarding how in-depth or how detailed your desires should be. They can be varied from a precise desire: *"I desire a job at Acme Computer Company in San Jose, CA as a software engineer, making $180,000 per year."* Or you can be more generalized: *"I desire a job as a software engineer for a company that is stable, has advancement opportunities and pays me a salary that is consistent with my qualifications."* You can even open your options up further by just desiring the feeling: *"I desire a job that allows* *me to utilize my knowledge and talents, that will pay me fairly and where I am happy."* How detailed your desires are is up to you, it's your choice. Keep in mind, the more detailed your desires, the more precise your manifestations will be.

When you are in the process of developing your desires, remember to present them in a desirable or high vibrational manner. Your desires are things that you want, not what you don't want. It is very common to think of things we don't want in our lives, which are undesirable things. If you have those thoughts turn them around into the opposite. For example, if you don't want to keep gaining weight, turn "I don't want to be fat anymore" into "I am now eating healthy and my body weight is perfect."

Write your desires into present tense "I Am" affirmations and really use your imagination.

Remember, these methods of asking are to be focused on one desire at a time. If you send mixed or multiple desires, you will receive mixed and often undesirable results. We attract into our life what we think about the most, so think about one true desire often and with true emotion. Know that you deserve it, and that it has already been manifested in your vibrational reality.

Remember, you need to maintain faith and a high level of vibrational energy. This is easily done by choosing to show and share your happiness, your gifts, your gratitude, and exercise your imagination by living "As If."

By living with an "as if" vision we mean to mentally take yourself to the level of manifestation you desire. If it's a new car you desire, picture yourself driving it, make a vision board, write affirmations about it, you can even go test drive one at the dealership. We refer to doing so in order to stay focused on your desire. Mentally living "as if" helps develop and maintain your high vibrational energy. There are several techniques and methods available that we have found to be very effective in maintaining your "as if" energy.

Vision boards are very effective in subliminally programming your subconscious mind. In fact, subliminal marketing is incredibly effective and used extensively throughout the world of advertising. Why not create you very own ad's and market your desires to your inner, subconscious audience? Vision boards are fun to make and fun to use. You can make them out of poster boards, and glue pictures and sayings to them. You can even create them with your computer. However, when you choose to make your vision boards, make sure they are visible and viewed frequently. All too often, we find something we like, and the first thing that pops into our mind is that it's too expensive or out of the price range. Now, stop for a second and think about what you just affirmed. You just declared a very low vibrational emotion of lack and unworthiness. As *like attracts like*, you now are in the process of creating or co-creating an environment or reality that will support your lack and unworthiness. Ah, the law of attraction hard at work for you! On your vision boards, affirm "I am always blessed with more than enough money to purchase anything I truly desire."

John Assaraf tells a great story about one of his vision boards. As he was moving into his newly purchased and renovated home, he was unpacking boxes with his young son. In one of the boxes there was a collection of some of his vision boards from years gone by. His son asked him "what are these, daddy?" John pulled out some of the old vision boards and started explaining the process to his inquisitive son. While looking at a vision board he made over five years prior, he realized that the house on the vision board was the very same house he just purchased and was moving into. Back then, when he created the vision board five years prior, he had no idea where this house was, what it cost or any other details. It was just a picture of a beautiful house he cut out of *Dream Homes* magazine.

There are many stories of people arranging their physical realities in order to accommodate their visionary or vibrational reality. Remember, everything in the physical manifested from someone's vibrational reality.

Living "as if" strengthens your faith and your belief and keeps making it stronger and stronger. Living "as if" allows you to feel and express all of the fantastic and joyous emotions your desire enhances.

The idea of living "as if" is the same as living with expectancy. When you are expecting a baby, you prepare for his or her arrival. You get all the necessary items needed to care for your baby and you excitedly wait for the special day. Before the baby is born, you are living "as if!"

Before you go on vacation, you visualize how fun your adventure is going to be. In your mind, you are already laying on the beach in Hawaii, or screaming down the Matterhorn at Disneyworld! This is living "As if!" You see it, feel it, live it and enjoy it, all while it is in your imagination, a.k.a, your visionary or vibrational reality.

It's the feeling of expectancy, knowing that it is already yours. Just like when you gaze at your presents under the Christmas tree or on the gift table at your birthday party.

Picture yourself in your imagination as having already achieved this desire. See yourself doing the things you'll be doing when it physically manifests, feel and enjoy the emotion. Lock in that feeling and enjoy it every time you think about your desire.

The other process we encourage is Affirmations. Affirmations are the strongest and most effective way to influence your core beliefs and alter your present reality. We are a product of our beliefs and our choices in life. Many of these beliefs were instilled in us when we were young; beliefs that have been passed down through family. These beliefs include, for example: religious practices, medical or health remedies, fears and superstitions and even cooking instructions. There is a humorous story about a woman who always cuts off the ends of the ham before she puts it in the oven. One day, when asked why she does that, her reply was, because that is how her mother cooked ham. Now, having her curiosity raised, she then asked her mother. The answer was the same. It turns out that four generations back, the woman's great, great grandmother had to cut off the ends of the ham because the roasting pan and the oven she had back then was too small for an entire ham to fit in.

The intention of an affirmation is to generate a specific emotional feeling spawned by the manifestation of the specific desire. By using your imagination, your words create mental images, which in turn create feelings or emotions. It's the energy from these emotions, or thought vibrations, which broadcast outward to both mentally and then physically manifest our desires into reality. As the Law of Attraction dictates, your resulting manifestations will match the feelings you get when saying your affirmations.

Starting and stating your affirmations with "I am" puts them into the present tense. By doing so, you're tapping into your "as if" imagination and will generate desirable feelings and emotions, such as joy, happiness love and gratitude. The result will cause a shift in your reality, thus manifesting your desire.

Affirming in the present tense ("I Am" vs. "I will") ensures that your subconscious mind immediately goes to work on creating an environment to manifest the desire. There is a great difference between saying "I will be so happy when ..." and "I am so happy now that...". Remember, thoughts create things, so if your thoughts are focused on "I will," then you will be stuck in a never-ending state of "I Will-ness," and your result will be a hopeful feeling for a better future rather than your targeted desired feeling or emotion generated by the manifestation of your desire.

Only use words that have desirable and high vibrational energy. Don't use low energy words like: *stop, quit, avoid, no longer or lose.* Avoid verbs and phrases that represent lack, such as: "*I want,*" *I need," or "I hope."* You should also avoid stating the "Problem" within your affirmation. Remember, <u>always affirm what you desire, not what you no longer desire</u>. You can use these low energy feelings as an indicator as to what you do desire. For example: you feel fat and want to lose weight. The affirmation "I am no longer going to be fat. I am losing weight every day" may sound desirable but is full-on nothing but low energy words and messages for your subconscious to lock into. A more desirable affirmation is: "I am happy to be living a healthy and active lifestyle. I am now only eating healthy foods. I am proud of my beautifully proportioned, fit and trim body."

Keep your affirmations as brief as possible. Your subconscious mind does not think in the same terms as your conscious mind. The subconscious thinks in mental pictures therefore short precise affirmations gives your subconscious mind the information and time it needs to convert the affirmation into a mental image.

Be sure to read them and recite them multiple times per day. You can write them down, print them out, make them your computer, iPad and iPhone background, hang printed versions throughout your home, make a wallet-sized version to carry with you, record them audibly into your I-pod, and read them, look at them, and listen to them over and over again, all throughout the day. This is how you generate a very high attractor factor!

You create the "What"

Let the universe create the "How" and "When"

This may sound a bit odd or tricky but the answer to "How do I get it?" is "it's already done!" The answer to "when do I get it?" is "it's already yours." When you were asking for your desire to be fulfilled, you already manifested it on your vibrational plain or reality, therefore, whatever it is that you are desiring has already been manifested.

As you learned earlier you must release any "need" for your desire and enjoy its vibrational manifestation while it's in your imagination. Once this is accepted in your subconscious, universal energy then start the process of physical manifestation. How it is done is the universes responsibility, not yours. Your "how to's" are very limited, while universal power is not.

If you look out your window right now, you will most likely see some trees. On average people see between 15 to 20 trees. So in this metaphor we use trees as our "how to's." So you have 15 to 20 "how to's" on your list. Now think of how many trees there are on the entire planet. According to NASA and Google Earth there are over 3 trillion trees on earth. So in essences the universe has over 3 trillion "How to's." Now compare that to how many trees you see out your window. Looking out your window is figuratively the same as looking at your "how-to" list in comparison to the universes "how to." That is why you don't have to worry about the how. You need only have the faith and belief in your higher source. And as for the when, that is also up to the universe.

By focusing on the "how" you only create worry and doubt, and you know they are very low vibrational energies. Your responsibility is to stay on the high vibrational plain, stay in faith and belief that your desire or something better is now being physically manifested into your reality. How long it will take, from our experiences, depends on the situation as well as your vibrational plane or level of consciousness. This is easily done by choosing to show and share your happiness, your gifts, your gratitude, and exercise your imagination by living "As If."

An old Chinese proverb states "A journey of a thousand miles begins with a single step." Before you can take that very first step you have to decide which direction you want to go in and where you'd like to go. Remember Einstein's definition of insanity as doing the same thing over and over but expecting different results? Having the desire points you in the right direction. Changing your route and taking that first step is the action necessary for achievement. A desire without self-motivated action is merely a wish with little chance of coming true.

Dr. Richard K. Nongard and R.J. Banks

SECTION 2:

CREATING YOUR BUBBLE

OF PROTECTION

Chapter Three:
Self-Protection

No one talks to you more than you do. The average person's inner monologue is about 150 to 300 words per minute. These internal conversations amass to over 50,000 thoughts per day. Our minds are also very efficient at internal multitasking, meaning you are reading the words in this book right now while evaluating, agreeing or disagreeing with its content, you may also be watching the clock waiting to pick up the kids from school, thinking about what to make for dinner, etc. This form of thinking is generated and formulated in the conscious region of your mind. Your reactionary thoughts and responding choices, both physically and mentally, are then transmitted to your subconscious region of the mind, and the reactionary process is executed. These are not two separate minds but rather two spheres of the same mind.

Your Subconscious mind is non-judgmental and has no concept of right or wrong, positive or negative, good or bad. Its job is to carry out the instructions sent from your conscious mind. This action is often compared to a ship's captain and his crew, with the captain being the conscious and the crew being the subconscious. The captain announces an order and the crew respond without question. They are simply following orders.

So essentially, anything and everything you say about yourself to yourself becomes an affirmation and declaration for your subconscious mind to insure these "desires" come to fruition. Remember, your subconscious has no gauge or barometer, it is programmed to follow orders. It is for this very reason that we always recommend people never to tease or joke around about themselves, their looks, their weight, their education; the list goes on. Even though you are joking, your subconscious does not know or understand the intention behind your words. It is open, working and taking orders 24/7.

More often than not, many people have become their own worst enemy; sabotaging success, imperiling abundance, and creating a spiraling sense of mediocrity or worse. When we recognize that the way to put in place a protective bubble to shield us from negativity in the world, we must first begin within ourselves. When we start from within ourselves, we are in total control and can quickly activate the APP to the promises of Advanced Parallel Programming and the Law of Attraction. The result will be a complete turnaround in your life. Instead of mediocrity, you can achieve excellence. Instead of self-sabotage, you can become your own compass — discovering new opportunities and new ways of aligning thoughts, feelings and actions with the Law of Attraction. Instead of being your own worst enemy, you will become your own best friend.

Much of the previous chapter was devoted to the foundations of the Law of Attraction. To create alignment between ourselves and the ability of this law to help us exceed our expectations and dreams, the first bubble of protection we must activate is the shield which will protect us from our own thoughts, beliefs, and negative alignments. The way to do this, using the APP metaphor, is to learn an important acronym. The acronym is C.O.R.E. and each letter signifies a potent solution in Advanced Parallel Programming.

C- Create a new way of talking to ourselves

O- Observe our existing self-talk

R- Replace old patterns of speaking to ourselves with new patters we have created

E- Expand our repertoire of positive self-talk

Like a fish swims in water, people swim in thoughts. A fish is always surrounded by water, in fact, without water, it will not survive. We in turn, are swimming in our thoughts, surrounded by them, both conscious and subconscious. This is where our self-talk comes from. Self-talk may exist in actual words and phrases we tell ourselves ("I'm not sure I can do this," or "I don't deserve this," or "I can't ever seem to get what I want.") or they may exist in simple nondescript feelings, awareness, or partial thoughts. Even though more abstract, these subtle influences deep within us guide our actions and create our realities. We often refer to these deep inner stimuli as intuition, gut feeling, and hunches, and they greatly increase the level of emotion. Often it is this self-talk, at a subconscious level, that is out of alignment and not parallel to our immediate goal of abundance, desires, or even our needs.

Create: We must create new self-talk; this must be deliberate. This is where affirmations, promises and visualization exercises can be of particular value. In fact, right now, as you read the pages of this book, you can pause, close your eyes and practice seeing yourself as you know you really are. See yourself as abundant, see yourself as strong, see yourself as one who takes action rather than waiting for an opportunity. It feels pretty good to do this, doesn't it? From this simple exercise, what promises and new realities can you tell yourself? Think about them. Can you create new counters to your negative self-talk? Simple things like, "I am determined," or, "I am strong," or "I manifest opportunity" are framed in a positive and affirming way.

Here is our Morning Affirmations mantra we both use, and a downloadable version can be found on our website:

37

Dr. Richard K. Nongard and R.J. Banks

Today is an incredible day. Success, abundance and prosperity in many different forms have naturally found their way into my life today. I gratefully enjoy these manifestations throughout my day and happily share these blessings of abundance with many others in order to help bring happiness to their day as well:

I Am Happy

I Am Healthy

I Am Wealthy

I Am Loved

I Am Secure

I Am Worthy

I Am Forgiving

I Am Forgiven

I Am Blessed

I Am Confident

I Am Courageous

I Am Excited about Today!

We recommend you print these out and recite them every morning, as well as throughout your day. This will help you stay focused.

Observe: Must of our self-talk, the internal dialogue we have with ourselves all day, goes unnoticed. This chatter, much like the background chatter in a restaurant, is not something we pay much attention to, and yet, it is always there. We must mindfully practice paying attention to this chatter. Discover what we are saying to ourselves. When you discover background chatter from within that is unhelpful, use it as a cue to return your attention to the moment and the positive self-talk phrases you have just brainstormed. Clinical psychologist Steven Hayes, Ph.D. recommends you think of those negative thoughts as "unruly passengers in the backseat of the car you're driving. You hear the noise and ruckus behind you, but you keep your attention focused on the road ahead."

This is the heart of creating lasting change, observing yourself and then without being hard on yourself, refocusing back to something resourceful.

Replace: To install new ideas, you must develop a plan, a goal, or an intention. Intention setting can be quite powerful. Unlike goals, intentions are not about the future, they are about the 'right now'. You can create hypnotic new ideas and use them as an affirmation on an index card, or as a spoken mantra. Try these on:

- I intend to be wealthy
- I intend to be healthy
- I intend to be wise

Use self-hypnosis to go forth from your observation sessions and into the day, acting on these intentions and you will discover the old misbeliefs cease to exist. One of my favorite pithy quotes is, "Think outside of the box, and the box ceases to exist." Self-hypnosis is a tool for doing this. It is what Napoleon Hill meant when he wrote, "Riches do not respond to wishes. They respond only to definite plans, backed by definite desires, through constant persistence."

Expand: Retraining our internal programming does not just stop the bad. It does much more than that. It brings us into alignment with the Law of Attraction and it expands our universe. The goal of Advanced Parallel Programming is expansion of our lives, so that we have something bigger than ourselves to share with the bigger world around us.

Although we have focused on self-talk as a tool for protecting ourselves from our own thoughts that are incongruent with the Law of Attraction, there are other tools we can use also for this self-protection:

1) Live non-judgmentally. Practice being gentle and forgiving to yourself first. You will discover this is a powerful way to then be gentle with others and forgiving with others. As we will discover in the last

section of this book, this is a vital component to sharing the power of the Law of Attraction with others.

2. Develop rituals that reinforce your desires. This can be as simple as taking care of your body, caring about your clothing, and starting and ending each day with a short meditation or self-hypnosis session. Setting your intention for the day is a very important.

3. Talk to yourself in the third person. According to a dual-pronged study published in Scientific Reports, "During times of distress or when you're reminiscing about painful experiences from your past, talking to yourself in the third person—by using non-first-person pronouns or your own name—can help you stay calm, cool, and collected without much additional cognitive effort." It is hypothesized that referring to oneself in the third person helps you think about yourself in the same way you think of others. Third-person self-talk leads people to think about the self, similar to how they think about others, which provides them with the psychological distance needed to expedite self-control.

    Remember, you are in control. What you say to yourself, or how you describe yourself to others, occurs through your conscious level of thought. Therefore, you have a choice. We are and attract into our lives what we choose to think, say and believe about ourselves and our perceived reality.

Chapter Four:
Protecting ourselves from
friends and family

Our spouses, partners, parents, children, friends, and co-workers are all people we undoubtedly hope will be our biggest supporters. After all, these are the people who are closest to us. These are the people we love, and the people who love us. While this is the way it is supposed to be, many of our closest allies actually work to sabotage our success. In most cases they do not do this out of malevolence. Sometimes it is out of jealousy, but more often it is because they harbor limiting beliefs and don't want to be miserable alone.

The singer Morrisey, famously wrote a song titled, *We hate it when our friends become successful.* The lyrics:

> *We hate it when our friends become successful*
> *And if they're Northern, that makes it even worse*

And if we can destroy them
You bet your life we will
Destroy them
If we can hurt them
Well, we may as well

When we understand that the old adage: "Misery loves company" is in many cases true, you can begin to see their lack of support for what it is – truly a desire to be comforted as *they* wallow in misery. Billy Joel also wrote song lyrics that directly addressed this idea in his song *Piano Man*, "Yes, they're sharing a drink they call loneliness, but it's better than drinking alone."

It is commonplace to have different values and beliefs amongst family members and friends, and that is okay. Careers, lifestyle education, partners, religion, and politics are all common reasons for these differing ideas. Although they mean well, it is also commonplace for one or several of these loving souls to inform you that "they" know what is best for you. Do not allow someone to treat you badly just because they are family or a "close" friend. Remember, this is your life and your decisions to make, not theirs!

To activate your APP Bubble of Protection at this level and create parallel alignment when surrounded by negativity from those who we would expect to be supporters of us, we should always approach this from a spirit of love, compassion and forgiveness. Although, in rare cases, a 'frenemy' might actually want to hurt us, nine of ten times it is really about their own self-protection. The acronym L.O.V.E. is how we activate our bubble of protection from those in our immediate world who are not yet in alignment with our values and the Law of Attraction. Keep in mind, everyone is at different stages in life. You would not expect a toddler who is just learning to crawl to get up and start running a marathon, would you?

L.O.V.E. stands for:

L- Love other people with genuine compassion and with a spirit of forgiveness. We must begin by mastering the art of forgiveness. One great strategy for this is the Loving-Kindness Mediation. The benefits of meditation are widely known, practiced worldwide and maintain high regards and respect throughout the ages. You may already practice the art; you may have tried it but couldn't get into it, or you just don't think it would be beneficial for you. But wait! Did you know there are many forms of meditation? There are visualization meditations, open-focus meditations, loving-kindness meditations, mantra meditations, and so many more. You just have to find the discipline that is right for you. We have found that Loving-Kindness Meditation is a very easy and effective form of meditation that we encourage you to learn.

What is Loving-Kindness Meditation?

Loving-Kindness meditation focuses on developing feelings of goodwill, kindness and warmth towards others (Salzberg, 1997). According to researcher Dr. Emma Seppala, Science

Director of Stanford University's Center for Compassion and Altruism Research and Education, compassion, kindness and empathy are very basic emotions to us. Research shows that Loving Kindness Meditation has a many benefits ranging from enhanced well-being, providing relief from illness and improving emotional intelligence. Here are a few of the benefits regarding emotional support.

1. Increases positive emotions & decreases negative emotions
2. Increases vagal tone which increases positive emotions & feelings of social connection
3. Activates empathy & emotional processing in the brain
4. Makes you a more helpful person
5. Increases compassion
6. Increases empathy
7. Decreases your bias towards others
8. Increases social connection

The effects of implementing a Loving-Kindness Meditation routine into your daily life is actually quick, easy with immediate and very effective results, even in small doses, and the results are long-lasting.

How to Meditate the Loving-Kindness way:

As mentioned earlier, there are several variations of mediation, and whether you are a pro at it of struggle just to stay focused for just a few minutes, we are happy to share with you our version of this meditation on our website at www.AdvancedParallelProgramming.com.

In her book titled: *A Return to Love,* author Marianne Williamson shares a very effective method of forgiving and letting go. It is as simple as repeatedly reciting: "I forgive you (whomever) and I release you to the Holy Spirit" (or Universe, or whatever your higher source is. Your higher power can even be your own inner resources and strength). R.J. Banks has been using this technique for many years and it has proven to be extremely effective in releasing undesirable feelings and emotions. He says that sometimes he only needs to repeat it for a few minutes, and other times he repeats it for hours. Sometimes it even takes days. He says you will know when it is released. A sense of ease and peacefulness fills your emotions and you smile. If those undesirable feelings ever start boiling up again at any time, you know what to do.

Another effective mantra to repeat to yourself in times of stress, anger and strife is: "No one is making me feel bad, I am doing it to myself. Therefore, I can choose to change how I feel, and I do so now."

O- Observe those close to you. Pay attention and adjust your actions accordingly. There is no need to deliberately walk into a hornet's nest. These are your people, your family, your close friends and in the spirit of keeping the peace, sometimes it's best to lovingly agree to disagree. Remember do not allow someone to treat you badly just because they are family or a "close" friend.

V- Vibrate at the highest levels of empathy, compassion, and support for those around you. Negativity is never countered with more negativity; it is always countered with love and compassion. The naysayers are usually the ones watching you the closest just waiting for that "I told you so" opportunity. But this is actually your opportunity to shine! Once they realize your progress, the tables turn, and you have a great opportunity to inspire them. Remember you have been educating yourself, working with and refining your skills and knowledge on this phenomenon, they haven't. The familiar term "Lead by example" holds very true when it comes to living on a high vibrational plane.

E- Evolve. By practicing these principles, you will evolve as a beacon of strength and your care for others will help them to evolve to a place of alignment. For some this will happen quickly, for others it will happen slowly, for others, the components of impacting others we will share in later chapters of this book will have to be activated, but in the end, we believe love always trumps misery.

Psychologist *Tara Brach*, founder of the Insight Meditation Community of Washington, explains it perfectly in her great metaphor: "Imagine you are walking in the woods and you see a small dog sitting by a tree. As you approach it, it suddenly lunges at you, teeth bared. You are frightened and angry. But

47

then you notice that one of its legs is caught in a trap. Immediately your mood shifts from anger to concern. You see that the dog's aggression is coming from a place of vulnerability and pain. This applies to all of us. When we behave in hurtful ways it is because we are caught in some kind of trap. The more we look through the eyes of wisdom at ourselves and one another, the more we cultivate a compassionate heart."

Chapter Five:
Protecting Yourself from a
Negative World

We live in an interesting time. Although that which is wonderful in the world surrounds us, we also live in some ways in a post-truth world. Social media, alternative media, and public messages are conflicting, and it does seem that political polarization is at an all-time high. Remember though, 200 years ago, political disagreement was solved with a pistol duel. We have at least made some progress. Social media, from Twitter to Facebook, and almost every other platform does seem inundated with opposing messages, unkind discourse, and bizarre appeals to the worst in people. Memes are shared that polarize, and a typical day on Facebook, especially during political seasons, seems to be a debate between those who know the least and feel a need to convince the world they know the most.

Many people love watching the news. When they tell that to other people the response is often, "That's crazy! The news is filled with nothing but tragedy, mayhem, manipulation, and plain old bad news." And while we do not disagree, Richard and R.J. have learned to reframed it. You see, something is news because it is unusual, odd, or rare. If it were not, it would not be news. As long as the daily newscast is filled with the tragic chaos that seems to mark each nightly broadcast, we know that such news is the exception. Bad things are not the normal state. The world still is a great place.

Believe it or not, and it might not feel like it right now, but our current world is healthier, richer, with less war and less destruction than any other time in world history. Imagine the day when the news will start with, "We have a special announcement: Mr. Jones baked a cake for his ill neighbor. In other news, a woman on the airport tram gave up her seat for a frail elderly passenger that needed to sit. And Carmen Smith, age 35, picked up the neighbor children after school so their parents could be together at an important doctor's appointment and the children would be able to eat ice cream with their friends after school." That is the day we need to actually worry. That is the day that the real news is that kindness, compassion, and empathy are the exceptions rather than the rule.

The first rule in protecting yourself from the negativity in the world around you is to choose to look for what is positive. It is there. It might not feel like it, but it is. A spiritual axiom is that whatever we seek we will find. If you seek that which is negative, you will discover it, but even by watching the tragedy of the evening news, you will find something good if that is what you are looking for.

The strategy of reframing, like we shared in regard to the lens through which we view the evening news, is a powerful way to protect ourselves from negative energy in the public consciousness. When it comes to people-powered social media though, such reframes can be more challenging. But there is a strategy. It actually can be applied to any form of social media, pubic media, alternative media and the negative messages and vibrations that are shared from church pulpits (for example, "you will roast in hell for eternity because of your desire to love certain people") to public information campaigns (remember how negative the "This is your brain on drugs" public information messages were? Or how "stranger danger" warnings used to thwart hitchhiking?).

Yes, there are negative messages, and they do influence us. They can induce fear, they can separate us from fellowship with other groups of people, and they can create a lack of congruence between the positive vibration of abundance we desire and strive for and those dark thoughts. We believe one of our purposes in life is to experience joy at every level. This means more than finding the silver lining in any cloud, it actually means living above the negative vibrations and in a parallel state to our deepest needs. This is Advanced Parallel Programming.

The acronym F.U.N. is a simple way to raise your level of joy and to once again align our vibration by influencing the Law of Attraction to a high level of joy and happiness. F.U.N. is a tool for helping you advance beyond the negativity and start living abundantly on your high vibrational plane. The best part? You don't have to wait for the results. The results are immediate!

F.U.N. stands for:

F-Friends. Those who lift you up. Social media gives you an opportunity to potentially engage with millions of people. There are more than 500,000 people who currently follow our social media group on Facebook (visit www.AdvancedParallelProgramming.com to link these resources where you can participate), and there are millions of people who have viewed our collective YouTube videos, and each of us has thousands of followers on our personal social media as well. Some of them are our childhood friends, with whom we have little in common with today, others are readers of our many books, and some are colleagues, family, or other acquaintances. Both of us have done something with intention though, as we have screened our followers and friends to some extent and have chosen to surround ourselves with positive people who contribute to our lives, rather than take from our joy.

Think now about your friends list. Are there people you dread who comment with divisive language and unhelpful or even hurtful comments? These are people we have chosen to mute or avoid or even unfriend when the discourse impedes on our happiness. You have the same options with alternative media, broadcast media, and messengers who pontificate divisive prose. Elevate your happiness by intentionally choosing which forums you participate in, what television programming you watch, and what messages you hear. Choose with intention to tune into those who are a beacon of hope, a trumpet of joy, and empower others, and change the channel from the crap that pollutes your mind and causes a misalignment between your values and beliefs.

If the music you are listening to glorifies violence, is misogynistic, and looks at the dark side of life, change your station if you desire to attract a joyful, happy and peaceful lifestyle. The great thing about living in a Pandora and Spotify world is now we can create our own playlist, and listen to that which builds us up. We always tell people they have a choice in what they listen to. You can choose to listen to "I'm a loser baby, so why don't you kill me" or "We are the champions of the world." Both songs are great musically, but one has a message that edifies the spirit, the other one, not so much. The same holds true with the violent video games you choose to play and the television shows and movies you choose to watch. To stay in alignment with your high vibrational plane, using the Law of Attraction means that you should curate the media you consume.

These are the five types of friends we encourage you to seek:

1. Those that inspire you
2. Those that are motivated and motivate you
3. Those that are open-minded
4. Those that are passionate
5. Those that are grateful

U- Unfollow negativity. You have absolutely no moral obligation whatsoever to "like, friend, or follow" anyone on any social media account, no matter who they are. Make the decision to unfollow any messages from the world around you that are hateful, harmful, or depressing. Your focus should be on quality not quantity, as body count is only an ego-driven concern. The Bible puts the Law of Attraction in these terms: "Whatsoever things are pure, whatsoever things are lovely, whatsoever things are of good repute, think on these things." This does not mean putting your head in the sand and avoiding reality. To the contrary, it means simply choosing which reality to listen to. Are you going to listen to a political message that says we are all just cogs in the machine and the elite control our destiny? Or are you going to choose to listen to a political message that empowers people to live their best life. The choice is yours. Unfollow that which harms you and contributes to misalignment, no matter what the source, or who the source of that message is. You can unfollow someone on Facebook and still stay friends with them. They will never know. Simply go to their page, locate the dropdown labeled

"Following" in the upper right of their header and click on "unfollow." By this action, you will still stay friends with them, but you won't see their negative or limiting content. And if you do choose to unfriend them the button for that is located in the same area of their page. Muting achieves the same on Twitter. We actually both unfollowed the President of the United States in our twitter accounts. We recognize the POTUS is important, and that direct communication from such a high political office is a recent phenomenon. But the vitriol on both sides of the political aisle makes any news feed from the highest office in the land a social waste dump. We choose not to have that in our lives, even if it's interesting. Instead, both of us have chosen to follow people who inspire and edify, like @guruguzzi and **@tinybuddha**. Both of these amazing accounts post great content that is sure to motivate you and keep you inspired. We encourage you to visit our Facebook page at: facebook.com/loaaffirmations. On our account, we post inspirational and motivational content, as well.

N- New relationships that align with your goals, desires, and highest thoughts. By choosing to unfollow that which is unhelpful and choose to nurture the friendships and relationships that contribute to your wellbeing, you have a golden opportunity. And that opportunity is to develop new relationships beyond the limitations of your existing network. In our Law of Attraction Affirmations Facebook group, we have over a half-million members who participate and contribute as well as those who are simply observers or readers. In order to raise your vibration and to align to a higher level of personal development, work on developing relationships that are non-toxic and contribute to your hope, happiness, and well-being. Maybe you are not getting the support you wish you had from the people on your personal newsfeed (we will share some ideas for changing that later in this book), but you are the one who is electing to stay in this negativity by also choosing to not connect with the many caring people who are using social media in a responsible way.

This triple-layered invisible bubble of protection is an amazing resource that can and will alter your life for the better. It will keep you focused on your desires using Advanced Parallel Programming and the Law of Attraction.

Remember: We are and attract into our lives what we choose to think, say and believe about ourselves and our perceived reality.

SECTION THREE:

ALIGNING WITH OTHERS AND

SHARING ABUNDANCE

Chapter Six:
Be the Change You Desire

Imagine a world where everyone is attuned to the same high vibration of attracting abundance, peace, wealth, compassion, and health. It would be a pretty amazing place wouldn't it? It seems that, in many ways, the world lacks congruence. Wars between nations are created and people often have competing interests. The result? Conflict, disagreement, and failure.

For as much progress as our civilization has made in the past 100 years, with the advent of new technologies and changes in every aspect of life from business to politics, we are, in many ways, still misaligned. Congruence between people and systems are lacking.

Like most of you, we have seen the bumper sticker that says, "Be the change you want in the world." That is exactly what this section of the book is about, how you can inspire others. This really is the "Advanced" part of Advanced Parallel Programming – taking it to the rest of the world. By hiding the light of the Law of Attraction so only we can feel its warmth, it might keep us safe from criticism or unfair judgment, but it also limits the real impact we can make by being a beacon of light for the Law of Attraction.

Neither of us are gymnasts, and you probably are not either, yet both of us have a real appreciation for the gymnastics events where the parallel bars are raised to a higher level as the competition goes into its final phases. That is what this section of the book does; it raises the parallel bar of your vibrational plane so that we can carry the message of hope that the Law of Attraction brings to the people you love, to the community you live in, and - because there is no reason not to think big - the world as a whole.

As you read through this section of the book, we will share with you ways to communicate on a shared vibration of abundance so that the people you love will want to join you in attaining happiness, fulfillment and joy. There is no greater feeling than knowing that the people we all love have also adapted a manner of living that produces happiness, security and significance.

We will share with you ways to engage your community. This includes the people you work with, the neighbors you interact with and the broader community of organizations and people with whom you fellowship. We are going to raise the bar in this section and create congruence, where in the past there might have been an absence of camaraderie, or even conflict. This is Advanced Parallel Programming.

In this section we share ways to impact the world. Is it possible? Consider that the flames of a thousand candles can be lit by the spark of one. It is possible. We know that such promises are a bold undertaking, but through mastering these methods of Advanced Parallel Programming, both your immediate world and the world as a whole will be a better place.

You will be learning how to effectively communicate with others in a compassionate and encouraging manner. You will learn how to teach, share and inspire others to better their lives and begin to be happier and more fulfilled. We will also share with you some incredible and amazing stories of success and triumph of the use of Advanced Parallel Programming and The Law of Attraction.

Before we flip the pages and venture into the next section of this book, take a moment to meditate on your connection to others. You can do this by simply reading these words and setting aside any anxieties about the future or your ability to persevere, and set aside any regrets of the past. Bring yourself fully into this present moment, holding the pages of this book and being exactly where you need to be at this time, doing exactly what you need to be doing to bring about change in the world.

Take in a breath, noting that each breath marks each moment and this moment is filled with your intention – your intention to advance to the higher parallel bars, and to align yourself with an even larger sphere of influence.

Read each sentence that follows out loud, and let yourself capture the energy of this moment:

> I ask for compassion
>
> I am compassionate
>
> I receive compassion
>
> I ask for wisdom
>
> I am wise
>
> I receive wisdom
>
> I ask for energy
>
> I am carrying this message to others
>
> I receive a world in return, filled with abundance.

Now turn the page and enter the next section of this book knowing that what you have learned will guide and help you to help others, which will make the world a far better place.

Chapter Seven:
Lead with Compassion

In the popular Peanuts comic strip, Lucy bestows therapeutic advice to the other kids from her "advice stand" for five cents. There is a reason her advice costs only five cents: It turns out advice isn't worth very much. It's not that the advice is not correct or that it won't work, but its value is diminished because the person who is on the receiving end of advice simply does not want it.

There may be many reasons why your advice might not be taken, and in many cases, the reason is pride. We're not talking about the pride you feel when you accomplish something wonderful, rather, we're delving into the undesirable and ego-driven pride. If you offer either solicited or unsolicited advice to help people activate the Law of Attraction, the results are often the same: It is soundly rejected. In order to accept advice, especially unsolicited advice, they must own their failures, inadequacies, and need for advice. People just don't like engaging in these aspects of themselves. It goes against our natural instinct for self-reliance and autonomy. Pride often keeps people from not only failing to act on advice, but can even cause people to actively work in an opposite direction than the advice suggested.

We know the Law of Attraction creates abundance, prosperity, and in the long-run, an easier path to success, problem-solving and creating the future we desire. Because of these successes, we are often tempted to offer advice to those in sphere, so they too can actively reap the benefits of the Law of Attraction. Advice, however, is not the best way to start bringing others into alignment with the Law of Attraction and the many desirable benefits it can bring into one's life. The alternative: Lead with compassion.

Compassion literally means "to suffer together." It is described as an emotion that arises when you are confronted with another's suffering and feel motivated to relieve that suffering. In this book, we identify suffering as living an unhappy and unsatisfying life, and through our understanding, we are motivated to share the power of the Law of Attraction.

Compassion communicates something powerful. It tells the people we love that they are as important to us as we are with them. By leading with compassion as a way of bringing others into alignment with the Law of Attraction, we are literally attracting people rather than advising people or try to sell them on a concept. The work that you will be doing in this section of the book to align yourself with the people around you should be work that is easy. It is far easier to attract people to the Law of Attraction than it is to advise people to get with the program.

One of our students is Joni. Joni is a 37-year-old single mother of two school-age kids. Joni learned about the Law of Attraction a few years ago by watching a movie which introduced her to some of the basic ideas. Since that time, she has been an active member of our forum (www.AdvancedParallelProgramming.com) and has grown immensely in her success. These successes include attracting abundance with her small yet thriving internet marketing company she started so that she would be able to work from home. She has also attracted the love of her life after a traumatic divorce six years ago. In her everyday life she has learned to be and stay positive, sharing basic strategies for looking on the bright side with her children, and being involved in her community. She has a definite plan for her manifestations, enjoys creating and sharing her vision boards with her kids, and is consistently creating, reciting and listening to positive "I Am" affirmations. You can say Joni is very attuned to the Law of Attraction and has what many call "a high attractor factor."

The challenge? Although her new relationship is going well, and they are great for and to each other in almost every way, he thinks she's a crack-pot for always "trying to attract" things into her life. At this point they are starting to actively struggle in their relationship because of his constant negativity. He is a wonderful person who is always taking the easy and secure path, rather than going for the more risky yet more rewarding pathway of stepping out in faith and self-reliance to create success. His business, a painting business, seems to always be having problems with payroll, mechanical failure in his trucks, and even personnel problems. The source of contention: Joni keeps giving Pete (her fiancé) advice. It is good advice, it's based on her matching entrepreneurial skills, experience, and successes in attracting health and wealth despite life difficulties. Her advice is well-meaning and comes in the form of "I think you should do this" type of communication.

Everything Joni has told Pete is great advice from a logical perspective. Her advice to buy a maintenance contract on his trucks is sound business advice. Her advice to hire two extra part-time student employees to cover any gaps in the schedule is right on target. Her advice to "keep looking up, not down." But all this advice is grating on Pete's nerves.

Why? Part of it may be pride, and part of it might just be familiarity with struggle. A lot of people really are stuck. The familiarity of failure, mediocrity, and difficulty actually can provide a sense of security for many people. This same illogical perspective is why children cry when they are taken from their abusive mother, or why the abused wife will defend the man she just called the cops on when they arrive to arrest him for beating her up. However, it really does not matter what the source of rejection is, Pete and Joni, however much they love one other, are not in alignment. They lack alignment because Joni, who is compassionate with her intention, has not lead with compassion.

When Pete comes over after a tough day at work, he has come home for compassion. He has literally come over so that he can be with someone he loves and just sit with them. If you have been in a situation like this, it is easy to dispense advice. In fact, we might even think that by giving that advice we are being compassionate. But compassion is about attending to someone first. It is about putting our hand on their shoulder in a non-shaming, non-sexual way and just *being* with them. Compassion is about listening, even if what we hear is clearly attracting the opposite of abundance. Sometimes people talk to us, not because they actually believe the misery they are spouting, but simply to have a sounding board. They are in need of someone to listen, and someone who is willing to accept them even if what they are saying is self-defeating.

After we listen, rather than giving advice, we can create alignment by turning that compassion into action by doing something with our loved one, rather than telling them what to do. What Joni learned in our group was that by leading with compassion rather than advice, she was opening the doorway to intimacy. Intimacy in this case, is a shared experience. Joni was with Pete in every aspect of his solution, and this was parallel alignment.

Joni stopped giving advice and started attending. She just listened. She gave her time, and showed that she cared. In fact, when our friends, loved ones, and colleagues come to us with negativity, what they are often doing is communicating to us that they value our presence and advice, but they just don't know how to show it or ask for it. We do, however, caution you at this juncture to not become someone's emotional dumping ground. You are there to inspire and share a wonderful and fulfilling way to live. We will discuss this in further detail further in this section.

Joni did four things differently to lead with compassion:

1. Joni listened and did not offer advice until she was specifically asked for it.

    a. It was out of her compassion that she previously was quick to offer advice, but by doing this before attending, it was rejected.

2. Joni offered her time.

    a. She was busy with her children and her business, but when Pete was flustered by another no-show, she volunteered to go finish the job with Pete. After the job was finished, late in the evening, Pete asked, "What am I going to do to avoid this again?" That turned out to be the right time to share the idea of hiring part-time students.

3. Joni modeled the solution rather than giving advice by asking Pete to help her solve a problem in her business that she knew was similar to issues he faced.

    a. By doing so, she activated his own inner-problem solving and she knew that the advice he offered to help her would become a self-fulfilling mechanism for his own application of similar solutions.

4. Joni led with compassion by being empathetic.

    a. She did this by avoiding judgment and responding only after she imagined how she would feel if she was in the same situation. By waiting to offer advice and practicing empathic listening, she began to notice a huge change in the quality of their relationship.

As we are writing their story, we are happy to announce that Joni and Pete are now in alignment with one other. Pete is participating our workshops and meetings with Joni, and we just received an invitation to their wedding.

The way to advance your parallel status and to get others to align with the successes of the Law of Attraction through Advanced Parallel Programming is by leading with compassion.

What are some other ways to lead with compassion? Joni and Pete are soon to be married. You probably find compassion towards those you are close to comes naturally. We can lead with compassion in almost any situation. In the workplace, we can lead with compassion in the following ways:

Sharing encouraging words. This is especially effective if you are a supervisor, as many employees perceive their bosses as focused on problems.

Coming alongside and helping others. Compassionate supervisors and coworkers can lead with compassion by helping others complete their tasks.

Take time to listen. It does not matter what your role in the workplace is, or if you are high or low on the 'totem pole'. Listening to others is always a hallmark of compassion.

Show kindness. Take the time to smile, to open a door, to help carry a box, or in any other way practice kindness in the workplace.

In our families we can show compassion in many similar ways. Compassion in the real world can be demonstrated in many of the same ways as well. Leading with compassion creates a curiosity in others. It creates a curiosity about our lives, and an improvement to our attitudes. It is then that we can share the Law of Attraction, from not only a base of compassion but with the authority that base has created.

Chapter Eight:
Share Your Story

What is your story? If you are passionate about the Law of Attraction you are probably one of the many people who came to it through a period of hardship and trials. If you read the section at the beginning of this book called *About the Authors,* you'll know that both of us have come through hardship and discovered abundance in many forms, and this is what drives us. We see others who are where we have been, and we want to share how our lives have been changed by Advanced Parallel Programming and the Law of Attraction.

R.J. Banks actually wrote his contributions to this book with dictation software. Why? R.J. is legally blind. Six years ago, after a long and successful career in both the music industry and then as a radiological imaging specialist, doctors discovered a brain tumor. Although he survived the surgery, the damage to his visual cortex has resulted in permanent blindness. R.J. now says he sees the world better through his heart than he ever did through his eyes. He has found abundance despite hardships in the years which have followed.

Richard gave a TEDx talk in 2019 that was largely based on his story of multi-generational alcoholism in his family and how he discovered how living fully in the present moment (Mindfulness) can change lives. In his book *Turn Around Trauma*, he shares his own experience in recovery from addiction. He shared what it was like, what happened, and what it is like now.

These are our testimonies, our testimonies to the power of creating alignment through Advanced Parallel Programming and how we have attracted abundance despite hardship as a result of the Law of Attraction. Today, R.J. enjoys his life and has the best guide dog on the planet, named Cabo, who he shares his life with. Today, Richard has broken the cycle of addiction in his family, and with 32 years of sobriety, his adult children have never seen him take a drink.

Both of us have come from difficulty and transcended the negativity in the world and surrounded ourselves with supportive people who live in harmony with the Law of Attraction. The results? In both of our businesses, families, and communities, we believe we have left a legacy of contribution. But the best news is that this is not something only we can experience, but something you can experience as well. R.J.'s career started in the Air Force, Richard began his career as both a pizza delivery guy and as a car salesman in college. Our families are similar, both of us came from families that had our basic needs met, but neither family was wealthy. Both of us experienced hardship, family traumas, as well as joys and support. In many ways it is probably similar to yours. What separates us from others is that despite the difficulties and negativity in the world, we both have held fast to the idea that our Creator wants the best for us, and that if one adheres to the principles of Ask, Believe, and Receive, the Law of Attraction is activated in our favor and puts into motion powerful forces that align our lives with abundance.

Both of us often speak at conferences and conventions, and we speak to community groups, companies, and social groups. We also speak to individuals one-on-one, sharing our stories and the Law of Attraction. By sharing, three things happen. First, it reminds us and reinforces for us that by seeking alignment and believing the best, we stay in alignment and reinforces these ideas. Secondly, through sharing our stories, other people learn from our experience. Other people will grow to understand that no matter how far down we might have gone, Advanced Parallel Programming can lift us up and keep us on track. Third, it ignites a curiosity in the lives of those we are speaking with. It causes them to look inside themselves and ask, "Is it possible that I can have what they have?" This is what excites us most about sharing our stories.

One story most are familiar with is that of actor Christopher Reeve. In 1995, he became paralyzed from the neck down following a horse-riding accident. Using his connections and influences along with his strong focus following the Law of Attraction, Reeve manifested multiple levels of Advanced Parallel Programming. Reeve orchestrated fundraisers in parallel with public awareness using his Hollywood influences, in parallel with contributions to medical research that is making great advancements to this day. He became very involved in programs that assist handicapped children and paraplegics. In 1998 he started the Christopher Reeve Paralysis Foundation and to date, the organization has raised over $138M. These contributions have changed thousands of lives, and that number is still growing. Although he himself was never able to walk again, his contributions to this cause as a whole are seen as a triumph and have been inestimable.

If you have seen the movie or read the book titled: *The Secret*, you may recall the story of Morris E. Goodman. Mr. Goodman is also known as "The Miracle Man," because he is one of the very few pilots in the world who has survived a plane crash. After his small twin-engine airplane lost power it came crashing to the ground. When the First Responders arrived at the crash site, they were amazed to find that Mr. Goodman still had a pulse. Once at the hospital, he was diagnosed with numerous injuries including his spinal cord being crushed and his diaphragm. He could not move any part of his body what so ever, except he could control blinking his eyes. His overall prognosis was that he would stay paralyzed like this for the rest of his life, and due to his diaphragm injury, he would never even be able to talk or breath on his one again. He, on the other hand, had a different vision. Using his knowledge of the Law of Attraction, he set his goals and intentions to someday walk out of the hospital on his own two feet. The only thing he focused on was recovering, and four months after the accident he began breathing and eating on his own, and eight months later, he did in fact walk out of that hospital on his own two feet.

Although these are big headlined making events, the Law of Attraction creates miracles and changes thousands, if not millions, of lives every single day. Lives like yours and ours. In our groups we always share, inspire and encourage one another. In our "show-n-tell" segments, our members share their manifestations as well as the path they took using Advance Parallel Programming and the Law of Attraction.

Tom and Susan B were both working and only had one car, and it was on its last leg. They began their manifestation process with Ask, Believe and Receive by using Advance Parallel Programming and the Law of Attraction, affirmations and vision boards. Soon after that they were both driving new cars - cars that are reliable, efficient, and well within their budget.

After a harsh breakup and divorce, Merry C. had made up her mind that all men were losers, or what we'll call "frogs." Focusing on the belief that one must kiss a bunch of frogs in order to find a prince and with the power of the Law of

Attraction always working, Merry would attract nothing but frogs. She was familiar with the law of attraction and even wrote down a list of desirable traits she'd like to find in a man. Unfortunately, Merry was not in line with her belief. She let the Universe know what she desired in a man, but then she let the Universe know that she believed there were no men in existence who carried those desirable traits. We are happy to report that ever since Merry joined our group, she has learned about Advanced Parallel Programming and has refined her beliefs and faith in men. Her desires and her beliefs are now in parallel alignment and she is excitedly waiting to meet her Prince Charming someday soon. In the meantime, she is living "as if" and is enjoying her life.

Our friend Laurie has a bit of a different story as she did not come from a place of hardship. Laurie has been blessed and happy most all of her life and just knew that's how life is supposed to be. She never really knew what to call this "power" that she possesses until she read the book *The Secret.* This enthusiastically opened her eyes to the world she had been unknowingly living in. She then began researching and learning all she could about the Law of Attraction and how it works. This is when she met R.J. Banks. At that time (pre brain surgery and blindness) he was broadcasting a weekly radio show on the LOA Radio Network and it was Laurie's favorite show. She then read his book; *The Power of I Am and The Law of Attraction,* joined their Facebook group and has been a beacon of success to many others. Laurie's story shows up that you don't have to come from a place of tragedy to improve the quality of your life using Advanced Parallel Programming and the Law of Attraction.

For you to create alignment in the world around you, you need to start sharing your story. In your own mind you may have a clear idea of how you have manifested through the Law of Attraction. Your story might even be dramatic. But have you actually taken the time to write it out? By writing, you make it real. Words create. There is power in writing your story.

The format for storytelling that has successfully helped the 12-step programs to thrive as a force for good. This format includes:

1) Telling where you came from and what it was like.

2) Telling what happened to change your course of action.

3) Telling what it is like now, after making the change.

You can read the story of Dr. Richard Nongard in the recent book, *Turn Around Trauma*, that uses this format. It is a simple and powerful storytelling format. It can create a short story, "I was broke and nearly penniless and learned to have faith, and now I attract abundance." Or it can be a longer story. My friend Rich Guzzi told me his story in this format when we first met.

Rich told me about struggling to understand the concepts in *Think and Grow Rich* by Napoleon Hill, reading it over and over again, but feeling like he didn't quite understand how it really applied. At that time he was struggling, trying to make a name for himself in the show-business world. One day, a panhandler hit him up for some cash as he walked to his car. Rich didn't have any cash in his pocket, but did have some bills in the car. He told the panhandler, "In a moment I am going to get my car in that parking lot, I have some money there, and I will drive around the lot and back to this corner and I will give you some."

Rich told me that by the time he got out of the lot and to the corner he the panhandler was already a block away and crossing the street. Rich had the money in his hand. The panhandler never got it because he did not have faith. He simply didn't take the abundance that was there.

Rich explains, "It was at that moment that I understood the book. From that point forward, the abundance I have experienced has wildly surpassed my expectations."

Be ready to share your story with others. Craft your message like a master storyteller, and share it one-on-one, in classes, social media and anywhere else you can get your story out.

Chapter Nine:
Lift and be Lifted

Set this intention right now: The intention to surround yourself with others who are aligned with abundance. In order to rise to the next level and lift up those around us, it is important that we have people lifting us up as well. The collective power of many is far greater than the power of one, not only physically but vibrationally.

When R.J. lived in Los Angeles back in the 90's he enjoyed going to watch the LA Dodgers Baseball team play. His most memorable experience was when he witnessed an incredible turn of events brought on by the collective vibrational power of many. It was the last inning of the game; the Dodgers were down by 2, there were 2 men on base with 2 outs. Stepping up to bat was the Dodgers worst hitter. It seemed grim and hopeless. The first pitch was thrown, swing and a miss. Then strike two. What happened next was incredible! All of a sudden there was a very noticeable shift of energy in the entire stadium. It was "towel" night so all the people in the stands were given small hand-sized Dodger towels upon entering. Then without any queue whatsoever, everyone in the stands stood up and started chanting the batters name in unison and waving their towels. It was an awe-inspiring sight; one R.J. will never forget. The collective energy was so strong with nearly 56,000 people all in parallel with one another chanting and waving their towels. The final ball was thrown, the batter swung the bat and for the first time, hit a home-run clenching a 1-point victory for the Dodgers. The crowd went absolutely crazy! The Dodgers won the game! The Law of Attraction is not meant to be kept or used in isolation. Rather its full potential is revealed when others help us set our sights high and when we use this energy to lift others up as well. You can think of it as setting the parallel bars higher for everyone.

Advanced Parallel Programming becomes second nature when you live in abundance with those who also live in abundance. Today, both of us are surrounded by high profile and successful people in business, our community, and as personal friends. This did not happen accidentally. Both of us have sought out others whose lives are filled with the joy of positive living, and by drawing from their vibration and energy we are able to lift up others. In fact, some of these people inspired us to write this book, a book we believe will lift up many. This is Advanced Parallel Programming and the Law of Attraction in action.

Remember, like attracts like. If you have struggled to feel supported in manifesting your desires, have you first manifested those who will support you? There is power in numbers. We can do things as a group, even a loose-knit group of associates, that we could never do alone. We can reach higher levels of financial success, manifest loving partners and friends, and even improve our health by being with other likeminded people.

Bill Gates will forever be known for both creating Microsoft and for being the richest man in the world during his lifetime. While both of these things are true and may eclipse awareness of his philanthropical contributions, Bill Gates has left a far bigger mark on the world through his funding of charities and projects that have solved very basic needs for millions of people. His work in Africa to fight Ebola has saved countless lives, and his pledge to provide tens of millions to eradicate polio might top the list. Gates has also been a significant contributor to ending hunger, HIV, ALS, and to help deliver health services to the least fortunate on our planet. He left his job at Microsoft to devote to philanthropy full-time.

Success came to Bill Gates early in life, but it was not success without help. Early on he chose his mentor wisely, and chose Warren Buffet to help him both in business and in philanthropy. Gates knew that long-term success would require he surround himself with other successful business people. He knew that to touch the lives of others in a meaningful way with his wealth, he would have to align himself with other philanthropists. Gates has credited Buffet with changing his thinking, and his problem-solving abilities. Buffet helped Gates; he was a mentor, and as a result, millions of others have been lifted out of disease, poverty, and despair by Bill Gates.

You do not have to be a famous entrepreneur or executive to impact others. The key, is to start helping others by being part of a larger network and surrounding yourself with strength. These people can be spiritual mentors, business mentors, and relationship mentors. If you come from a family where unhealthy relationships were modeled, the way to make your relationships strong is to find relationship mentors who can help you. In turn, you will also lift those you have relationships with.

We all need mentors. We need strategic mentors, financial mentors, relationship mentors and spiritual mentors. Do find them, set the intention. Ask for people to be attracted into your life that can teach you. Believe that those people are interested in your life, and be open to receiving the guidance they will freely share.

This will put you in a position to lift others as well. It has been said, "show me your friends, and I will show you your future." The idea behind this expression is that we receive from those we associate with, and reflect those traits into the lives of others. Research even backs this, and in a surprising way. The famed Framingham Heart Study revealed that if a friend

81

becomes obese, you are 45% more likely to gain weight in the next few years. But what is really shocking, is that if a friend of a friend become obese, even if you don't know that friend, your chances of gaining weight increases by 20%. But wait, there is more: As crazy as it sounds, if a friend of a friend's friend becomes obese, you are 10% more likely to gain weight than to randomly gain weight.

The data from this study was comprehensive; it spanned thousands of people, and 30 years. They discovered, if your friend smokes, you are exponentially more likely to smoke. This is the Law of Attraction in action, and to create a parallel program – one in alignment with your goals and ideas – you must surround yourself with people who are on the same high vibrational plane you desire to be on and have what you desire. The research is in, living by the Law of Attraction is one of the fastest pathways to abundance, one that puts you parallel with your desires and actions.

Do you want wealth? Associate with wealthy people. Join networking groups, the Chamber of Commerce, and seek-out relationships with wealthy people, just like Bill Gates did. Do you want health? Associate with healthy people. Join a gym, sign-up for a tai-chi class, or start becoming involved with a community of healthy people. Do you want to be healthy and lift up others? Volunteer to be a youth soccer coach, to referee games in your local school and discover that success and abundance is always surrounded by success and abundance. Both R.J. and Richard volunteer their time to non-profit programs. Being blind, R.J. volunteers at the local blind center and Richard volunteers his talents with the local Best Buddies International organization, which create opportunities for people with intellectual and developmental disabilities.

In many ways there is truth in the words of Jim Rhome who claimed that we are the average of the five people we spend the most time with. Evaluate whether your current circle is helping you or hurting you. If they are hurting you, it's time to purge them. The good news here is that it is unlikely that we'll need to cut those closest to us out of our life, rather, we will be lifting *them* up by finding good people to lift *us* up.

We recommend you start by writing down a list of those closest to you. We are not *necessarily* just speaking of close family and friends; we are referring to anyone in your life you interact with on a regular basis. Granted, there are situations that you can't control, but there are many you do have control over. In fact, there are many situations in your life where you actually do have control. We've already discussed social media, but there are also physical social interactions that you have control of. If you don't like the service at that restaurant, stop going there. The same goes for where you choose to shop, fellowship, get your car serviced, and local social organizations. If these places and organizations are not parallel to your beliefs, then stop going and stop participating.

Once you have purged your current list of friends, you can then begin attracting new friends that are in parallel alignment with you. There are several ways to do this. We recommend you start by writing down the traits you desire in a true friend. Once you have established these parameters you can start affirming their manifestations and start visualizing being surrounded by like-minded people.

There are several social media groups on the internet that you are welcome to join. Our online groups are always filled with fresh new and uplifting content. Face-to-Face interaction is also a very important part of the equation. Again, we refer you to the internet and search for local Law of Attraction groups that meet regularly. Most cities have a local meetup.com website you can look through. We have been actively involved in LOA group meetups, Abraham-Hicks group meetup, The Secret meetups etc. It is very refreshing and inspiring to be running at the peak of Advanced Parallel Programming with so many likeminded people. You can also think about starting your own LOA Mastermind group, either online or as a live meetup.

Next, we advise that you monitor your own negativity and stay cognizant of your emotions. It can be easy to let negativity sneak into your life if you're not careful, and once you start attracting on this low vibrational plane you will be attracting more negativity, including negative people. Remember, We are and attract into our lives what we choose to think, say and believe about ourselves and our perceived reality.

If you want to attract positive people into your life, show your love to everyone. Smiles are very contagious. As the Beatles sang, "All you need is love, love... love is all you need." There are countless ways to show and spread your love every day. Stranger or not, if you see someone who needs help, offer them a hand. Show your appreciation to a coworker, partner, store clerk with an unexpected thank you note or card. Find something to compliment people on, even if it's an article of clothing or jewelry. Remember the Golden Rule? It says, "Be nice to others." It truly applies here.

Dr. Richard K. Nongard and R.J. Banks

Section Four:

Make the World a Better Place

Chapter Ten:
Teach Others

People only know how to do what people know how to do. Unfortunately, schools today are so busy teaching to the test that they are missing what is really important. In a world where we can find any fact with the computer in our hands, schools are still stressing rote memory of facts. In a world where complex mathematical equations can be solved in a millisecond by simply plugging the variables into a computer, kids are still being taught formulas. If you were a school board member and proposed learning creativity, Law of Attraction, emotional intelligence, financial literacy, nutrition and communication, you would likely be railroaded out of town. After all, these aren't the things measured on standardized tests.

Because 100% of our students graduate from both High School and college without ever learning these essential skills, young adults are sent forth with the ability to regurgitate facts, but without the skills of Advanced Parallel Programming. They simply do not know how to set an intention, create alignment between themselves and others, and they lack the ability to manifest health and wealth. They do not know how to properly care for their bodies, and our obesity rates continue to climb, along with the diseases that accompany them. They do not know that wealth can be guaranteed in old age by the law of compounding and simply saving money. An 18-year-old kid who saves $55 a week until they are 65 will amass over a million dollars. Because of the law of compounding they will have only put in $31,680 over the course of their lifetime. Considering the scale of the meager amount put in and the massive amount paid out, it is almost free money, and that presumes that no additional savings are made during the course of a lifetime.

To share the Law of Attraction requires that we teach others the power of the law. Both of us teach a lot of classes. Classes on self-hypnosis, classes on the Law of Attraction, and classes on many other topics and skills (you can find out upcoming course schedule at www.AdvancedParallelProgramming.com). What we have discovered is that by teaching others, two amazing things will happen. First, those we teach are empowered. They become excited by finally learning the skills that lead to success. Our teaching lifts them up. People leave our classes and seminars and start businesses, discover lasting love, and achieve their goals. We regularly hear from people who were stuck, took our practically oriented classes, and now feel unstuck.

The second thing that happens when we teach? We learn as much from our students and from the process of teaching as they learn from us. The axiom that both the teacher and student benefit, is a perfect example of the alignment that we are seeking from Advanced Parallel Programming. It is important to note, this teaching does not have to be in the form of an academic class, a seminar or workshop. You have the ability to teach people without desks and chairs, you can teach people informally, one-on-one, and you can teach the people you work with, share a community with, and the people you love the most!

How do you teach? You can teach in many ways. One of the best ways to teach is by example. When you model alignment, and when you model manifestation, people will notice and they will ask you. This gives you an opportunity to actually mentor and teach others.

People regularly ask R.J. "How can you be blind and have such a great attitude?" They are genuinely curious how one can have such a great physical limitation and yet unlimited passion for life and to seemingly attract that which is good despite a difficult situation. People ask Richard all the time, "How do you find the time to write more than two dozen books, run your training company, travel the world, and raise your family?" They are genuinely curious how Richard's "Life without Limits" can exist when their world is limited, their opportunity stifled, and their passion zapped. These are their self-limiting beliefs that you can help them change!

By modeling parallel programming, you attract curiosity, and you will effortlessly find people to share the Law of Attraction with and be able to each apply the skills of APP. Your co-workers will ask, your children will ask, your spouse will ask, and so will random people you encounter who need to have what you have.

Now the question is, what do you teach them? There are many elements of the Law of Attraction to teach. We often teach the formula: Ask – Believe – Receive, which we discussed in chapter two of this book and in R.J.'s book: *The Power of I Am and the Law of Attraction*. We also teach the basic concept that "focus equals fuel," and other basic tenants of understanding how the law works.

In addition to these basic tenants, you can also teach the skills of Advanced Parallel Programming. If it is true that people only know how to do what they know how to do, it follows therefore, that to be an effective teacher we need to go deeper into the Law of Attraction. One resource we can recommend to take your skills to a deeper level is the book, *Practical Law of Attraction* by Victoria Gallagher. We think it is the single best resource out there for advancing your alignment skills.

Another great resource is the book *Mental Chemistry* by Charles Hannel. This book is so important that we want to give you a digital eBook for free! All you have to do to get it is visit our website at AdvancedParallelProgramming.com (it really is free, just tell us where to send it and you can get a copy today.) Charles Hannel was a successful writer and businessman, who Napoleon Hill credited with his success as a result of the principles Hannel wrote about in his books.

There are four keys to abundance that Hannel wrote about in his book, *Mental Chemistry*. We use these elements as a solid foundation for our Advanced Parallel Programming. You should be sharing these principles with everyone who wants to know about your success. But in order to teach them, you must commit to learning these principles and commit to taking them to an advanced level. By doing so, you will reach a higher vibrational plane in your ability to align with the world around you and the results, like compound interest helping a kid make a million dollars from a $31,000 investment, will astound you.

We have been practicing these principles in our lives. We have seen our students practice these principles, and we know that by going deep you will manifest abundance, health, wealth, and success at both a faster rate than you previously have, and with compounding levels of desired outcomes.

Introductory courses in the Law of Attraction, and popular movies and books often build on the same themes. These ideas from Hannel, who arguably has done more to share the secrets of the Law of Attraction than anyone, are things you should learn, and things you can teach.

1.) Abundance is the natural law of the universe.

It always amazes us when people are victims of a scarcity mindset. Jealousy comes from scarcity thinking, fear comes from scarcity thinking, and depression comes from it too. Many people we encounter can easily reverse their course in life by learning a central truth to the universe: That the universe is abundant, and that abundance is the natural law of the universe.

One of our favorite texts from the Bible recognizes the abundance of the world.

"Therefore, I tell you, do not worry about your life, what you will eat or drink; or about your body, what you will wear. Is not life more than food, and the body more than clothes? Look at the birds of the air; they do not sow or reap or store away in barns, and yet your heavenly Father feeds them. Are you not much more valuable than they? Can anyone of you by worrying add a single hour to your life?

"And why do you worry about clothes? See how the flowers of the field grow. They do not labor or spin. Yet I tell you that not even Solomon in all his splendor was dressed like one of these. If that is how God clothes the grass of the field, which is here today and tomorrow is thrown into the fire, will he not much more clothe you—you of little faith? So do not worry, saying, 'What shall we eat?' or 'What shall we drink?' or 'What shall we wear?' For the pagans run after all these things, and your heavenly Father knows that you need them. But seek first his kingdom and his righteousness, and all these things will be given to you as well. Therefore, do not worry about tomorrow, for tomorrow will worry about itself. Each day has enough trouble of its own. (Matthew 6:25-34)

These principles of abundance outlined above resonate both with people of faith, and people who do not share a Biblically-based faith. Why is that? Because the principle is universal: The universe is abundant and this is the natural law of the universe. What this means is that we can claim abundance, we can give up on scarcity thinking, and we can manifest abundance. Sickness is sickness because it is not the normal state of our body. Poverty is poverty because the natural order opportunity creates is wealth. Depression is depression because joy is the natural order of abundance and these are things we can claim from our universe.

In his book *The Power of I Am and The Law of Attraction*, R.J. explains in detail how to correctly create your affirmations in order to keep them on a high vibrational plane. He, like most of his collogues, advises us to not use any low vibrational or negative words such as "stop, quit, lose, remove, etc." So, instead of affirming what you *don't* want, affirm what you *do* want.

A great example of maintaining positive wording for money is: "I am always blessed with more than enough money for everything I desire, and grateful that all of my needs are divinely care for." This affirmation tells your higher source that you understand the universe is abundant and you are blessed. It also tells your higher source that you do not worry about your needs and that you are grateful they are cared for. This is what the previous bible verse was saying. We feel that if you "need" something, you are putting out the low vibrational energy of lack. If you "need" something, you are lacking something and that tells the universe it is not doing its job correctly, that you have no faith or trust. The universe is abundant, you are worthy and there is more than enough for everyone.

How many gallons of water are in the ocean? 352 quintillion gallons is the answer. Did you think "quintillion" was just a made-up word? It is an actual mathematical number, and it's so big we cannot even comprehend its size. How much money is in the world? $5 quadrillion dollars is the value of the earth according to astrophysicist Greg Laughlin. $5,000,000,000,000,000.00 That is a 16-digit number. Our scarcity mindset is so small that we think the sun is big. But the Milky-Way galaxy contains over 200-400 billion stars, and over 100 billion planets. Some estimate there might even be a trillion stars! Each star is a sun. The Milky way is but only one galaxy. The one we live in. But there are probably over one hundred billion galaxies, each with billions of stars, and billions of planets.

The point is, there is a lot of everything. There is a lot of joy, there is a lot of wealth. There is a lot of health, there are infinite loves, infinite lives, and infinite opportunities. Discard the scarcity mindset and embrace the real abundance present in the universe. The more we discover the more infinite the universe becomes, and you are a part of this abundance.

If your scarcity thinking in your love life has you upset that you have not found "the one." It is time for you to realize that out of seven billion people currently living, you have not found "the one" *yet* because you have not looked.

If scarcity thinking in your financial life has you upset that you don't have enough money, then you have probably not been looking hard enough for your money. One million dollars is 0.00000033...% of the money just in the United States. You don't need a very big slice of the pie to have a lot!

The Law of Attraction works because the universe is infinite and you are a part of it. Think about this for a moment, your problems are small. They might feel big, but that is because we are small. Our unlimited potential comes from the fact that we are part of something bigger. This is the advanced part of Advanced Parallel Programming again. Thinking bigger, and realizing our ability to align with that which is infinite. Nicholas

Tesla said, *"My brain is only a receiver, in the Universe, there is a core from which we obtain knowledge, strength, and inspiration."*

Charles Hannel said it this way:

> "The Universal Mind is not only intelligence, but it is substance, and this **substance** is the attractive force which brings electrons together by the law of attraction so they form atoms; the atoms in turn are brought together by the same law and form molecules; molecules take objective forms and so we find that the law is the creative force behind every manifestation, not only of atoms, but of worlds, of the universe, of everything of which the imagination can form any conception."

Wallace D. Wattles was another deep, creative parallel thinker:

> "There is a thinking stuff from which all things are made, and which, in its original state, permeates, penetrates, and fills the interspaces of the universe. A thought in this substance produces the thing that is imaged by the thought. Man can form things in his thought, and by impressing his thought upon formless substance can cause the thing he thinks about to be created. In order to do this, man must pass from the competitive to the creative mind; otherwise he cannot be in harmony with the Formless Intelligence, which is always creative and never competitive in spirit. Man

> may come into full harmony with the Formless
> Substance by entertaining a lively and sincere gratitude
> for the blessings it bestows upon him."

Wattles also ties in the Advanced Parallel Programming with:

> "…make the most of yourself, for yourself, and for
> others; and you can help others more by making the
> most of yourself than in any other way."

When you know these truths, you can teach these truths.

2.) Thoughts + Actions = Parallel Programming.

It is not enough to "Name it and claim it." Faith without action
to turn belief into experience is dead. What many people miss
in activating the full potential of the Law of Attraction is
action. When our thoughts and our actions are in alignment,
we have created a parallel program. When we do this, we step
away from misalignment and into alignment.

Again, you have to know this to teach this, and by teaching this
basic principle of alignment you help others see the real
potential of Universal Law. If I think of wealth, if I think of
high dollar cars, fancy houses, and big paychecks, they can only
become reality if my actions are in alignment. Without saving,
I cannot create wealth. Without work, I cannot amass fortune.
Napoleon Hill, in his book *Think and Grow Rich* required not
just the thought of accumulation, but an action plan to create
it.

To discover lasting love requires that I leave my house, take risks, meet new people, and open up to the possibility of love. These are the actions that manifest a soul-mate, and these are the hallmarks of alignment.

You must become an expert in creating action. It is not enough to hope for health, wish to be thinner, and wish to have more energy. Your actions must be in alignment with your thoughts. You must eat right, you must walk on a daily basis, and you must choose actions that put nutrient-dense foods in your body before you eat nutritionally empty foods.

What do you want to manifest? By purchasing this book, there must be something you have thought you wanted, at either a conscious or subconscious level. We have good news for you. The universe is abundant, and you can manifest it, but these thoughts must be accompanied by action. This is what creates satisfaction with the outcomes. Putting everything in place using Advanced Parallel Programming means to have these factors in alignment with one another:

Focusing on what you desire.

Understanding your needs are already cared for.

Accepting that you are worthy of anything you desire.

Manifesting your desires in your mind.

Mentally feeling the true joy and gratitude upon receiving your desires.

3.) How to create ANYTHING: Imagination, visualization, and concentration.

Albert Einstein is quoted as saying: "Imagination is more important than knowledge. For knowledge is limited, whereas imagination embraces the entire world, stimulating progress, giving birth to evolution."

Nothing exists today that was not first a thought in someone's imagination. Thoughts are what become real. If you think depressing thoughts, depression will become real. If you think happy thoughts, happiness will become real. The table where you are sitting did not create itself, it first was an idea. The house or apartment where you live, the car that you drive, all of these things had to be an idea first in order to become a reality.

Thoughts create things. No matter what you want to create you can. You will do this by imagining, visualizing and concentrating. Charles Haanel tells us, ""By far the greatest discovery of all the centuries is the power of thought." and that ""Thought is energy. Active thought is active energy; a concentrated thought is a concentrated energy. Thought concentrated on a definite purpose becomes power."

Psychologists tell us that we have at least 50,000 thoughts per day. Like a fish swims in water, people swim in thoughts. Most of these thoughts do not come in the form of complete sentence or obvious awareness. Most are partial thoughts, subconscious awareness's and observations, and are mostly incomplete. Like the waves in the ocean, our thoughts are often simply flowing without a purpose or a direction. To create, we must harness the power of these thoughts, and that is done through imagination, visualization and concentration.

Imagination is perhaps, one of the greatest talents we as people have. It gives us the ability to problem-solve, to see things from a new perspective and to find creative uses for our thoughts. Kids are experts at imagination, but somewhere along the path to adulthood, must of us stifle the power of our imagination. We have responded to hypnotic messages to "stop daydreaming" and to "do as we are told."

As practitioners of the Law of Attraction we need to learn how to use our imagination, and then teach others how to benefit as well. We can learn how to use our imagination by becoming a child again, by letting go of the limiting negative self-talk that we have bought into. A simple strategy for imagining is expressed in the acronym O.P.E.N.

O – Observe

> It is important for us to observe any thought, situation, object or idea, and to see it not just as it is, but how it is connected and a part of the world around it. This

opens our imagination to connectedness. We can see how such ideas can be brought into alignment.

P – Possibility

Imagination looks at the misalignments and seeks to bring them into a parallel state by evaluating the possible combinations of related ideas. It is beneficial for you to practice seeing how one thing can come into alignment with another, how one thing can complement another, and how one idea can be shared in a way that aligns with another idea.

E – Envision

When we envision these alignments, we are literally envisioning a state of parallel programming. By creating a representation in our mind of these alignments, we are imagining a new experience, new ideas, and new things.

N – New Ideas

The new ideas that come from this process are the outcome of our imagination, and these new ideas will become our new reality. Give yourself permission to step back from old limiting beliefs and step into new ideas with new possibilities.

Visualization is the pathway to creation because it gives us a concrete representation of the imagination. Spend time in your meditations not just thinking, but visualizing. Here are some things to visualize:

- See yourself as you know you will be.
- See the things you want to acquire.
- Visualize things that are out of alignment moving into alignment.
- Visualize outcomes and your connection to the people you care about.
- Visualize in detail not being satisfied with a quick metal picture, but study your visualizations taking time to be with them.

At this point, many begin to wonder just how they are going to accomplish all their abundant desires. How answer is: Don't worry about the how. Remember, focus equals fuel. Where your attention goes, energy flows. Let the universe guide you to the how. Remember the trees analogy earlier? This is part of Ask-Believe-Receive. Ask for guidance, ask for a way, ask for the right people to come into your life, ask for the right opportunities to manifest in your life. This puts you into alignment so you can visualize all of these things coming into your life.

The brain does not discriminate between real and visualized experiences, we will respond either way. The easiest way to illustrate this truth is by thinking of a lemon. Right now, as you read the words on this page, visualize a lemon, and imagine cutting into its rind with a sharp knife. Imagine slicing it in half and taking half of that lemon and brining to your lips. As your lips feel the rind where you sliced and your tongue touches the tart fiber and you taste the sour juices from the sliced lemon, notice what is happening. Are you salivating? You have just produced a real response, and actual physical response, just from visualizing. When you visualize you create reality. Visualize love and you will find love. Visualize security, and you will find security. Visualize significance and you will be significant.

Any idea that we want to bring to reality is an idea we must concentrate on. Far too often, in our sea of thoughts, we simply move from one thought onto the next. Have you ever forgotten something that yesterday seemed so important? This is because we fail to concentrate on these ideas. We must devote our sticky notes on our computer monitor or refrigerator or by committing to an idea and enlisting the support and participation of others who will then hold us accountable.

If you want the Law of Attraction to work, understand the requirement for concentration. Emil Coue said, "Every one of our thoughts, good or bad, becomes concrete, materializes, and becomes in short a reality." Learn this principle of the Law of Attraction and teach it to others. Soon, the process of creation by imagining, visualizing, and concentrating will become second nature and will be a skill that serves you well.

Ester Hick suggests that if we can maintain focus on one positive and desirable thought for just seventeen seconds, we will trigger another thought on the same high vibrational plane. Link that seventeen seconds to the next seventeen and so on, and now you're flying high on your own high vibrational plane. Practice this technique during your meditation time. If you don't have a meditation time, create one!

3.) Thoughts are infinite and in this is great power.

Like the sand on the beach or the clouds in the sky, thoughts are infinite. There is no limit to what you can think. Old thoughts lead to new thoughts, and new thoughts lead to more thoughts. The power in this comes from the fact that we as people have unlimited potential. This is not a platitude; this is a fact. Your joy in life is that of abundance, even if life has hardship. Your success is abundance, it can be measured in a multitude of ways. In fact, if you struggle with not feeling successful, recognize this feeling probably comes from the limits you have placed on defining success. If you expand your thoughts, you will discover success is not something you will hope to have, but on some level, it's something you have already acquired.

When we commit positive thoughts, thoughts in alignment with your desires these thoughts become the foundation for subconscious replication of success. You will discover than in time, you do not have to try to find love, try to manifest wealth, or try to be your best. It will come automatically.

One can understand the action of the conscious and subconscious minds by observing the process by which the child learns to play the piano. He is taught how to hold his hands and strike the keys, but at first, he finds it somewhat difficult to control the movement of his fingers. He must practice daily, must concentrate his thoughts upon his fingers, consciously making the right movements. These thoughts, in time, become subconscious, and the fingers are directed and controlled in the playing by the subconsciousness. In his first months, and possibly first years of practice, the pupil can perform only by keeping his conscious mind centered upon the work; but later he can play with ease and at the same time carry on a conversation with those about him, because the subconscious has become so thoroughly imbued with the idea of right movements that it can direct them without demanding the attention of the conscious mind.

This is the great power of thoughts, the ability to commit processes and patterns of parallel programming to the subconscious mind. Consider these words from Charles Hannel:

> All things are the result of the thought process. Man has accomplished the seemingly impossible because he has refused to consider it impossible. By concentration men have made the connection between the finite and the Infinite, the limited and the Unlimited, the visible and the Invisible, the personal and the Impersonal.

Great musicians have succeeded in thrilling the world by the creation of divine rhapsodies. Great inventors have made the connection and startled the world by their wonderful creations. Great authors, great philosophers, great scientists have secured this harmony to such an extent that although their writings were created hundreds of years ago, we are just beginning to realize their truth. Love of music, love of business, love of creation caused these people to concentrate, and the ways and means of materializing their ideals slowly but surely developed.

Throughout the entire Universe the law of cause and effect is ever at work. This law is supreme; here a cause, there an effect. They can never operate independently. One is supplementary to the other. Nature at all times is endeavoring to establish a perfect equilibrium. This is the law of the Universe and is ever active. Universal harmony is the goal for which all nature strives. The entire cosmos moves under this law. The sun, the moon, the stars are all held in their respective positions because of harmony.

They travel their orbits, they appear at certain times in certain places, and because of the precision of this law, astronomers are able to tell us where various stars will appear in a thousand years. The scientist bases his entire hypothesis on this law of cause and effect. nowhere is it held in dispute except in the domain of man. Here we find people speaking of luck, chance, accident, and mishap; but is any one of these possible? Is the Universe a unit? If so, and there is law and order in one part, it must extend throughout all parts. This is a scientific deduction.

In this lengthy chapter, we have articulated four key points that will advance your understanding and practice of the Law of Attraction. These are things you should learn not just by rote memory but through experience. Discover applications of these principles and observe them at work in your daily life. Then share these ideas with others. Teach them in classes, teach them online, teach them to your children, your partner and your coworkers. Teach them to your community, teach them to strangers, and teach it to as many people as possible. The results will astound you, and direct your path towards a parallel program that creates alignment between you and others in the world around you.

Chapter Eleven:
Fine-Tuning Your Law of
Attraction Skills

"The vast majority of people are born, grow up, struggle and go through life in misery and failure, not realizing that it would be just as easy to switch over and get exactly what they want out of life, not recognizing that the mind attracts the thing it dwells upon."
- Napoleon Hill

When you teach people concepts, like those discussed in the previous chapter, you create enthusiasm and acceptance for new ideas. You remove limiting thoughts and create infinite possibilities. You must then seize the power of the moment to encourage skills development in the practice of Advanced Parallel Programming. Skills are repetitions of a pattern; they are the practice that makes perfect. Although the number of skills that you can teach others is also infinite, there are four important skills you should practice in your own life; These skills are:

- Creating incantations
- Mindfulness
- Setting intentions
- Releasing scarcity and negativity at every opportunity

Creating incantations: We were reluctant to use the word incantation here, but it is the right word. Incantation has the connotation of magic words that create. Sometimes, it is even associated with particular forms of religion and occult practices. It is the right word though, because words create, words are powerful and words have magic. Words can start wars, end relationships, heal trauma, and motivate people to make amazing changes. Words cast spells. We are not talking about spells with the intention to hurt somebody, rather, we are talking about the words that inspire and invoke desired change.

We should be giving ourselves incantations, repeating over in our head the positive actions we will take, the beliefs we want to hold, and incantations that open us up to receiving abundance. Even affirmations as silly as Stewart Smalley's "I'm good enough, I'm smart enough, and doggone it, people like me!" can be powerful. By creating incantations, we are reversing the language of mediocrity we have created in our self-talk, and we are able to step into abundance.

Mindfulness – The Great Master Oogway (the turtle from the Kung-Fu Panda movie) said it best, "Yesterday is history, tomorrow is a mystery, all we have is the present and that is why it is a gift." One of our biggest problems is the mind trap of either ruminating over past mistakes or missed opportunities. The truth is, we cannot undo the past. The past is what it is, and it is history. It is true that the past brought us to exactly where we are today, but now that we are here, this is the only moment we actually have any power over.

The other mind trap that we face is the minds constant tendency to attempt to predict the future, fearing the future, or anticipating the future. By focusing on the future, we often miss the this present moment. Many people teach the Law of Attraction as if it is something that will happen. The truth is, it is already happening. We can be healthy, wealthy and wise right now. If you are sitting in your apartment with bills piling up, fatigue and a lack of energy, feeling like you have made big mistakes, it is hard to see yourself as healthy, wealthy, and wise. But you are. Claim it for this moment, and be mindfully aware of what is 'right' rather than dwelling on what is 'wrong'. This is a powerful shift in thinking, and it requires practice. Our minds are primed to constantly scan our experience and to predict the future, so we are actually up against nature by learning to live fully in the present. But the present moment is the only moment we can impact, and practicing mindfulness is a skill you should develop. It will reduce anxiety, end self-defeating behaviors, and release you from the constraints of either past regrets or future worries.

Mindfulness requires is practice. The daily practice of mindfulness. Just like an athlete must practice for the game so that when under pressure during the big race they can perform at their best, we must practice mindfulness so that we can perform in a way that is best. By practicing, we are changing our brains, putting space between us and our thoughts, and preparing to step into a new chapter of life where we respond to everything differently.

To make mindfulness real you must want to change. By reading this book to this point you have clearly made that decision. Now commit to practicing mindfulness each and every day. The good news here is that unlike the gym, mindfulness does not take hours of practice each day. And unlike the gym that requires we get in our car and drive to a special place with weights, aerobic machines, and Zumba classes, we can actually practice Mindfulness anywhere and at any time.

We have never had a client yet who thought these beginning strategies were life-changing or profound when they first began. But the clients who did trust the process and follow our instructions for 21 days, almost always at some point came back with a huge smile, recognizing in retrospect the value of the practice.

They say that sharpening an ax does not fell a tree. But by sharpening the ax, it is far easier to fell the tree.

The idea of Mindfulness and staying in the moment might sound simple, but these are skills that need to be taught and practiced. It is not something that happens organically just by going to therapy once a week. A big part of the homework that we assign to my clients is to practice two minutes of Mindfulness, with intention, every day between now and their next session. And by the way, that's the great thing about Mindfulness. It's not about meditating for thirty minutes while assuming special postures or wearing unique clothes. In fact, a person doesn't even need to be still to practice Mindfulness. You can mindfully shop at the grocery store. You can mindfully walk. You can mindfully be still in a chair for some time, and you can mindfully eat raisins. Mindfulness is not about a specific style or vantage point of meditation, and it certainly is not about clearing one's mind. The goal in Mindfulness is not to empty one's mind or to stop thinking. On the contrary, the goal of Mindfulness is to simply give us the time to allow ourselves to observe ourselves swimming in our thoughts, in the present moment.

A Basic Mindfulness Meditation

While you could read volumes about Mindfulness, the best way to learn about it is to experience it. We will provide a script like the process I use with my clients; to truly learn about Mindfulness, you should, with intention, practice Mindfulness every day, twice a day for the next seven days. That's the same assignment that we give our clients, and we guarantee that if you do the assignment then you will find what our clients find: When they cultivate Mindfulness, the value of it is incredible.

Like an athlete or musician, practice is for a performance. Mindfulness meditation is our daily practice for living life to its greatest potential.

There are three components to the practice:

- First, the practice of directing your attention to your breath.

- Second, practicing how to return your attention to your breath anytime you notice feelings, thoughts or sensations. The goal is not to stop thinking, stop feeling or to stop having sensations. The purpose is to simply note when you do this and to practice bringing your attention back to a focal point, in this case, the breath.

- The third part of this practice is to begin to notice how easy and natural it is to stay in the present when we notice our attention drifting into either the past or the future. Notice, during this week, times when you mindfully and intuitively return from distressing thoughts, feelings, or sensations back to your breath into the present.

As you sit in your chair with your body relaxed and your posture in alignment, close your eyes and breath in, noticing what it feels like to breathe in.

Scan your body and loosen any muscles that are holding tension. Relax the jaw and let the shoulders drop and you can let your eyelids and hands feel heavy with relaxation as you just breathe. You don't have to try to speed up or slow down the breath during this exercise. All you need to do is breath and pay attention to your breath. There's not really a right way or a wrong way to do this practice. It is simply the practice of bringing your attention to your breath when you notice it wandering off.

Observe the breath, noticing the tempo of your breath, the temperature of the air, and the way you breathe. Observe how the air flows in, and what it feels like to flow out. We breathe every moment of the day, most of the time without noticing it, and by practicing paying attention to it, we are really practicing attention to this moment. Each breath marks each moment, and the only moment we actually have is this movement. No matter what stress we have endured, or are now enduring, at a basic level as long as we're breathing in this moment, we're okay.

As you breathe in and out, label the breath. Call it by its name. Label the in-breath "in" and call the out-breath "out." Say to yourself, "in" and "out." Notice the air as you breathe in and the point where the air in your lungs turns around and becomes an exhale. As you pay attention to the breath, you'll also notice you are aware of sounds, sensations, and experiences of your present moment.

The practice is not to stop noticing those things, but rather, when you notice thoughts and awareness's outside of the task of paying attention to the breath, simply note what you are doing and return your attention back to your breath.

If you notice yourself thinking about anything at all, you don't have to try to stop thinking; rather just note the thought instead of following it. Simply say to yourself that "this is a thought." Bring your attention back to the breath. If you become aware of an emotion or a feeling during this time, it's okay to have them. The practice here is not to suppress them, but not to follow them, to simply note them and say "that is a feeling" and return your attention to the breath.

Likewise, if you have any sensations, if your body feels something, you can simply note, "that is what my body feels, that is a sensation or experience," and without becoming engaged in it or following it just use it as a cue to return your attention to the breath noticing what it feels like to breathe in and out. Over the next two minutes, continue to breathe in and out paying attention to your breath. By practicing being an observer of the breath, you can apply this skill of observation to your traumas, to your adverse life experiences, and see them from a distance rather than 'being' your traumas.

The practice is of course to simply note when your mind begins to follow a thought or a feeling or an awareness of sensation and to gently, without judgment, return your attention to the breath. It doesn't matter if you need to do this many times. The value is in developing the practice of returning to this moment by returning your awareness to this breath.

Spend about two minutes doing this and then pay attention to what happens next; reorienting yourself to the floor below you, the air in the room around you and opening the eyes.

Note: Access a video and audio practice of this at AdvancedParallelProgramming.com

Although almost everyone can see the value in this exercise, most will discover the real value comes with practice. During this week, as you practice this exercise, begin to be aware of and notice when you intuitively practice Mindfulness and mindful awareness of the moment and other situations. For example, if you're stressed in traffic, you might notice when you become aware of the stress that you can automatically focus on your breath rather than letting the stress become a thought you follow. By the end of your first week of practice, you'll notice how natural and easy it is in a variety of different situations and places to mindfully focus on one minute at a time, one moment at a time, one breath at a time.

For the next 21 days, practice this daily, two to three times a day. We can promise, the daily practice will sharpen your ax. It will wire you to the present moment. It will give you a new strategy to stop the wandering mind from becoming anxious about the future or ruminating about the past. It is the practice that activates the potential, not the knowledge of it.

Setting Intention: Have you been setting your goals, failing to reach them, and then have become frustrated with goal setting? For many people, they mistake Advanced Parallel Programming with goals setting. In fact, we don't even advocate goal setting! When we share this with people, they often report that they have learned SMART goal setting, a particular type of goals setting that is widely advocated in corporate work, sales training, and personal improvement seminars. When we delve into the research on goals setting though, we discover that setting SMART goals might not actually be that smart. So, what is the alternative? After all, isn't it true that if you aim for nothing, you will hit nothing?

A better skill to develop than goal setting is intention setting. When we develop this skill, we will look back at the periods where previously we used to set goals and realize that any goals we would have set were wildly surpassed with intention setting.

Goals have several fundamental problems. First, goals are almost always based on what we want in the future. But as Master Oogway taught us, the future is a mystery. We really don't know what the future holds, and the only experience that actually matters is the right now, because this moment is reality. Second, goals are almost always based on what we think others want, or what expectations we think we are supposed to have based on how others will measure our success. Goals might be targeted, but they are almost always targeting consciously or subconsciously at what others want. Third, goals can create a spiraling trajectory towards mediocrity. Our natural inclination as we get towards our target date is to justify why we have not reached our goal and to revise them down so that we can feel a sense of accomplishment. This psychological principle is often overlooked in goal training courses, and this is one reason many people who set goals feel dissatisfied even when they reach their goals.

Intentions, on the other hand, are immediate. You can set the intention to be healthy right now, even if there are problems with your physical condition. We can set the intention to be wise with money, even if we don't believe we have enough. We can set the intention to be wise, even if we have made mistakes in the past. Do you see the difference? I can be healthy, wealthy and wise right now, and by doing so right now, I create the likelihood that in the future these elements will exponentially grow.

Intentions are owned by us. Nobody can say "I am" except you. Unlike goals, we have full ownership of intentions. I can intend to be happy, joyous, and free, but nobody can intend this for me.

Release scarcity thinking and negativity: Releasing negativity is a skill. This is a skill we should develop and a skill that requires practice. Once we master this skill, we can share it with others. This will bring us into alignment with those around us and create the resource of parallel programming that makes the Law of Attraction work in the lives around us.

We have enough within us to solve any problem. The practice here is to recognize the language we use which contributes to scarcity thinking and negativity and use affirmative language. This is the skill of seeing the glass as half-full rather than half-empty. You do this by practicing to develop an affirmative manner of living. It takes practice. Both of us believe we are skilled in this area, and do our best to live by this creed; however, there are times when we are more challenged than others. In fact, just this morning Richard picked up R.J. his dental checkup. R.J. was told he needs thousands of dollars of dental work, that it would be painful, and that the process would be time-consuming.

When Richard arrived to pick him up from his appointment R.J. was irritated. Irritated by the poor bedside manner of the dentist who did nothing to alleviate the immediate problem, irritated by the outrageous prices quoted, and irritated by the hassle he would be facing. R.J. related his experience to Richard, and his response: "What the dentist was actually telling you was that you get a Mexican beach vacation in Puerto Vallarta!" Richard shared my experience just a few weeks earlier having emergency dental work while on vacation in Mexico. It was the best dental experience he has ever had and what he saved more than paid for the four-day beach resort vacation.

By incorporating Marianne Williamsons forgiveness technique you learned in chapter two, combined with Richards compassion, by the time they arrived for their lunch meeting to discuss progress on this book, R.J. was feeling great, having released that negativity, and was ready to start looking for flights and booking hotels! Sometimes we all need an understanding friend to help us realize and release these undesirable low vibrational emotions. This is the compassion we described at the beginning of this book. This is helping bring someone back into alignment using Advanced Parallel Programming. A great book we highly recommend reading is *Don't Sweat the Small Stuff, and It's All Small Stuff* by Richard Carlson.

Here is another great visualization technique to release low vibrational negative energy. When one thinks of getting rid of something, we usually refer to that something as in the physical world. We either see in the real physical, or we picture it in our mind. Let's use a painting for example. You can walk around the room physically hanging it in various location looking for the best spot to hang it. You can also perform this task mentally. Either way, you are focusing on a physical object in a physical location. These are tasks and processes our minds are conditioned to perform normally. Emotions, however, are nothing you can physically see, smell, taste, touch or hear, therefore they are intangible and many people find it challenging to control or release them. This is why many people say they just can't 'grasp' something intangible like an idea or an emotion. A valuable point to remember is that these are your emotions. You own them, they don't own you. If you find it challenging to control a negative emotion, turn it into something physical first. Here is a technique we use and teach people to help them release these stuck emotions:

First stand with your eyes closed and your hands palmed out in front of you. Now visualize that negative, undesirable energy as a big ball of goo you are holding in your hands. Mentally look at it and understand this is the mass of undesirable emotions and energies that you pulled out of you that no longer serve you. It is now time to release them. With your eyes still closed and the ball of goo still in your hands, visualize yourself at a very high physical location. This could be a mountain top or cliff, or it could be a tall skyscraper building. The important thing here is to use your imagination and visualize the undesirable emotions as something physical you are holding in your hand and you are seeing yourself in a physical location. Now include your other senses as well and feel how hot and sticky that big ball of undesirable yuck feels in your hands. And the smell is so bad you can't hardly stand it. Even the thought of tasting it almost makes you nauseous. Now imagine you are standing with your back to the edge and proclaim: "I now release this undesirable energy that no longer serves me." Next throw that ball of goo over your shoulder and over the edge. Now, turn around and watch it falling away from you, getting smaller and smaller and smaller until it is gone, completely vanishing from your existence. Now take a deep breath and thank the universe.

There are several techniques that have been developed over the years for removing undesirable energies and refocusing on the desirable. There is no right or wrong way to do this. The best advice we can give you is to keep an open mind, learn about and try the various techniques, refine them and create a method that works best for you.

Chapter Twelve:
Action Steps

Although this is the last chapter of this book, this is not the beginning of the end. This chapter sets off the end of the beginning. You are no longer a Law of Attraction beginner. From this point forward, you are moving into a higher level of awareness that puts everything into universal alignment. By combining Advanced Parallel Programming with the Law of Attraction, you create a harmonious bond on a very high vibrational plane. Another one of Albert Einstein's famous quotes is: "We can't solve problems by using the same kind of thinking we used when we created them." Once you commit to making these changes, they will become second nature embedded into your subconscious.

How to apply & incorporate Advanced Parallel Programming into your daily life

Your first level of Advanced Parallel programming is with yourself:

As elementary as it may sound to some, living by the golden rule is a good start.

- o By helping others, you help yourself.
- o By teaching others, you teach yourself.
- o By loving yourself, you love others.

Notice on this last phrase we said to love yourself first.

The relationship you have with yourself sets the base or foundation of how you treat others as well as how others see and treat you. It is imperative that you show self-love all the time. Though like any other relationship, your relationship with yourself has good days as well as challenging days. This is where Murphy's Law can play tricks on you. We are all human and from time to time, we all make decisions or choices that are not congruent with our overall desires. We may even say or do something out of frustration. Remember, these are *your* emotions. You can choose to control your emotions and not allow them to control you. But remember, focus equals fuel, and where your thoughts go, energy flows.

More often than not, your low self-esteem and low self-worth are stemmed from past programming from outside sources that just aren't or weren't true. If you believe yourself to be unworthy, then somewhere in your life you were presented with the idea that you are. Eventually this idea became a belief. Although it was a lie, perhaps you were convinced because people you trusted told you so, or perhaps circumstances confirmed it to you. Regardless, the belief that you are unworthy was stored away in your subconscious as a truth. Now, your subconscious causes you to live in a way that confirms your lack of self-worthiness to be true. The power of your subconscious mind is the reason low self-worth can have such a destructive hold on you. It's something so ingrained in you that you unknowingly make decisions limited by the self-sabotaging deceptions of your subconscious. Casting out those old self-destructing beliefs and developing new thought patterns will do miracles for your life.

In her book *The Game of Life and How to Play it*, Florence Scovel-Shinn suggests you go to the root of where this negative belief began. Perhaps it was during your childhood, your marriage, first job, or a party in college. Visualize that moment in your mind. Then confront it. Be bold, speak out loud, **"Although this moment happened to me, the belief I made about myself is not true. It is a lie. The truth is (*fill in an awesome comment about yourself here*)."** Think it. Speak it. Shout it. Every day. It takes time, frequent correction and consistency.

We suggest you write down and then affirm out loud:

"I am _____. Anything conflicting with that statement is a lie."

Suggested adjectives to fill in the blank: *Worthy, Deserving, Confident, Valuable, Loving, Lovable, Smart, Beautiful, Funny, Honest, Strong and Secure, Courageous, Successful, A Winner, The Best, Interesting, Respected, Friendly, Kind, Compassionate, Forgiving, A Wonderful Person, Always Positive. Secure in Who I Am.* Remember, **good or bad:** *We are, and attract into our lives, what we choose to think, say and believe about ourselves and our perceived reality.*

Another interesting technique to release low vibrational energy toward yourself and to others is the ancient Hawaiian practice of forgiveness called Ho'oponopono, where one repeats the words "I'm sorry, please forgive me, thank you, I love you."

Author and Therapist John Kim says: "When you get to a place where you like yourself, the action of loving yourself will come more naturally. You'll have non-negotiables. You won't tolerate certain behavior from others. You'll seek less approval. Your friendships will be less lopsided. You won't have as many holes to fill within yourself. You'll be gentler to yourself, more forgiving. You'll believe you deserve more, deserve better, deserve different. You'll finally stop breaking the promises you've made with yourself. And the relationship you have with yourself will improve.

Here are some affirmations for self-worthiness, forgiveness and love:

I am worthy of a happy and abundant life.

I am always attracting positive and desirable people into my life.

I am always attracting positive and desirable opportunities into my life.

I am always radiating self-love and love for others.

I am forgiving of myself and forgiving of others.

I am worthy of a great and wonderful life.

I am free to be me.

I am completely in acceptance of who I am.

I am happy and allow myself to have fun.

I am happy with myself and my life.

I am a good person who deserves to be happy.

I am at peace with my past.

I am in control of my thoughts and emotions.

I am happy, healthy and wealthy.

I am self-love.

Your second level of Advanced Parallel programming is with Gratitude:

It is often said that the quickest path to abundance it through gratitude. We 100% agree. Constantly expressing your gratitude shoots you into a very high vibrational plane, and as long as you maintain this level of awareness, you will maintain a high attractor factor. The more grateful you are, the happier you will feel. Not to mention, sincere gratitude also opens the door to abundance! If you want to attract incredibly desirable things into your life, start by showing your gratitude, love and appreciation to all the people and things you already have around you in your physical existence. You should also show your gratitude to the Universe for the things you have only manifested in your mind. This lets the Universe know that you have already accepted these things as yours and that you are grateful for them.

There are a few methods of showing your gratitude on a daily basis. Firstly, always show your gratitude to the people you interact with on a day-to-day basis. Whether it be a friend, family member, co-worker, or stranger, always stay cognizant of showing your appreciation to everyone. This act of showing your gratitude and appreciation to others will always keep you on this high vibrational plane.

Another daily gratitude exercise you should incorporate into your new daily routine is by starting a Gratitude Journal. The practice of journaling has proven to be a very effective method of self-therapy, and in reference to gratitude, we find it just as effective and rewarding. We suggest you make two entries into your gratitude journal every day. Once in the morning and once at night just before you go to sleep. In the evening, think of three to five events that happened to you on this day that you are grateful for. This is sure to put a smile on your face when your head hits the pillow. This keeps you on in high vibration and in parallel sync while you sleep. We strongly suggest you slip into slumber with peace, love and gratitude rather than watching the 11 o'clock news, filled with stories of death, disaster and destruction. We also strongly recommend you do the same exercise in the morning. When you first wake up you will still be on your high vibrational plane by proclaiming your gratitude the night before. You can then carry it forward to start your day with gratitude and continue into your new day on a high vibrational plane. This time write down three to five things you are grateful for in your life. They don't have to be big life-altering events, you can be grateful for anything! You can even the air that you breathe. Ester Hicks of the famed Abraham-Hicks teachings say all you have to do is focus on one good thought for only seventeen seconds. When you do this, it sets into motion your opportunity to think of another vibrationally good thought for another seventeen seconds, and so on. This is a fantastic method of meditation. Once you get into the practice of living in gratitude and growing higher and higher on your vibrational plane using the seventeen-second method, you will unquestionably and undoubtedly create noticeable changes in your like.

<u>Here are some affirmations for gratitude:</u>

I am thankful for all of my blessings.

I am grateful for my life.

I am grateful for my healing abilities.

I am grateful for my abundance and prosperity.

I am grateful for my wealth and abundance.

I am grateful that I can help others financially.

I am grateful for the positive loving people in my life.

I am grateful for the opportunities I am blessed with.

I am grateful for the Law of Attraction.

I am grateful for this opportunity to teach and inspire others.

Your third level of Advanced Parallel programming is with Happiness:

We cannot stress enough how important is to be and stay happy, no matter what. Remember, Advanced Parallel Programming means staying in sync with all the other elements of the law of attraction to manifest your true desires. Being and staying happy will keep you moving in the right direction. Keep in mind that you are being watched by those you wish to inspire. If you have something they want, they will watch closely and learn what they can from you. Yes, we are all human and we have our challenges, misfortunes and bad days, but remember, you are in control. You have the capability to control your emotions and you may choose when to address any of these low vibrational issues when the time is right

On a scientific level, the physical and emotional act of being happy releases serotonin, endorphins, dopamine and other feel-good indicators throughout our body. In fact, just the simple act of smiling releases endorphins! Yes, that's right! When your mouth and face muscles create a smile, your brain reacts to the smile by saying "yippy, we are happy about something, let's party!" and the happy juices begin to flow, thought vibrations increase, and you are now attracting on this higher plane. Starting right now, start smiling, and keep smiling! Start a "smile routine" where every hour you remind yourself to smile for at least one minute. As a great training aid, get a pen or pencil, and place it longways between your teeth horizontally touching the corners of your mouth and then lightly bite down on it holding it in place with your teeth. This will physically stimulate the same muscle sequence as smiling, which will send the "party time" happy signal to your brain, and voila, you're now feeling the neurochemical reaction! This part of your brain has no perceptive thought process only a neuro-biochemical reaction response to the muscular stimulation.

<u>Here are some affirmations for Happiness:</u>

I am happy.

I am positive in all situations.

I am blessed with good things happening every day.

I am joyful, enthusiastic and motivated.

I am happy and allow myself to have fun.

I am happy with myself and my life.

I am a good person who deserves to be happy.

I am always sharing my smile.

I am always sharing my joy and happiness.

I am happy to inspire others my knowledge of the Law of Attraction with others.

Your fourth level of Advanced Parallel programming is your knowledge, and sharing of it with others:

The message you share and how you share it is your next line of parallel programming. The message you share must be the message you live. People in this day and age have grown privy and tired of the double standards many political, religious and business leaders live, get exposed, and expect us to accept. The last thing you want to do is fall into this category. Learn all you can about the Law of Attraction and keep learning. There are four basic concepts of learning.

1. Unconscious Incompetence

    a. You don't know what you don't know.

2. Conscious Incompetence

    a. You are aware of what you don't know.

3. Conscious Competence

    a.   You are aware of what you do know.

4. Unconscious Competence

    a.   You have mastered the task and execute it with ease.

Some of the most effective learning tools today are audio affirmation programs and audiobooks. You can listen to them day and night, in the car, on your break, when you sleep, and the list goes on and on. By listening to audio affirmations and audiobooks you are choosing to program your subconscious with pure positive high energy. Listen to as much as you can as often as you can. Learn as much as you can as often as you can and keep sharing. Once you reach your level of unconscious competence, you can easily share your experiences but simply being you. Living the life, your desire inspires others! You will find that by living by example many people will approach you. Remember that compassion, understanding and leading by example are your best resources when it comes to sharing your message about the Law of Attraction. Now is your time to shine! Go teach, inspire and live the happy life you deserve and desire.

WE CLOSE WITH THE FAMOUS QUOTE BY HENRY FORD:

"WHETHER YOU THINK YOU CAN, OR YOU THINK YOU CAN'T - YOU'RE ABSOLUTELY RIGHT."

Do you want free resources, recordings, and additional reading to help you attract abundance?

Are you looking for a motivational speaker for your next event that will not only bring a mindset of abundance to your group, but also leave them with the practical skills to take massive action?

Visit Dr. Richard K. Nongard and R.J. Banks at:

www.AdvancedParallelProgramming.com

Access the free resources we have provided, including one of R.J. Banks bestselling audio programs, for FREE!

You can also contact us with any question, and gain access to our private Facebook group from a link on our website.

AdvancedParallelProgramming.com

Made in the USA
Coppell, TX
18 March 2022

74929243R00090